1

Loving Like Christ

Loving Like Christ

How to Love the Hard to Love People in Your Life

Nelson L. Schuman

Dedication

To everyone in the world that desires to love more like Christ and to all who are in relationship with people who have been hurt by the enemy and need an extra measure of grace by someone who sees them through God's eyes.

<u>Endorsements</u>

"I have known Nelson since 2014 and have never met another man who loves people more like Christ as he sacrificed everything to help people that have been hurt by the enemy. He is truly a man of God that pours his life into hurting people and helping them change from a life of pain to a life of gain. His heart for people is amazing. He knows how to love like Christ loved the church and walk in His compassion."

Tim Brown – Sr. Pastor, New Life Assembly of God,

Noblesville, IN

"We all have people in our lives that, at times, have made it difficult to walk in love toward them. We have all been that person at one time or another as well. Nelson has walked the path carved out by the Word of God and the Holy Spirit, and has proven out that the love of God conquers all and causes real life change for the better that we could never have done ourselves."

David Natali – Sr. Pastor, Turning Point Ministries,

Carmel, IN

"This book helps to clarify why loving others can be a process. It is a guide to remaining passionate in our desire to love our neighbors as ourselves. May you embrace these insights in your journey with Christ."

Owen Mason – Sr. Pastor, Church Alive,

Lafayette, IN

<u>Testimonies</u>

"Loving people like Christ loved the church is what all Christians are called to do. The insight and wisdom that are inside this book are so important in getting the Lord's people to actually walk in His love."

"I had suffered much in my life with having to endure living with a spouse that was hard to love. After reading this book it taught me that it is a privilege to endure hardships for Christ and that He is changing me to becoming more like Him every day. I can do all things through Christ who strengthens me."

"I was married to my wife for twenty years and it unfortunately became harder for me to endure all the constant strife and complaining. I was ready to divorce her and end my misery until I was told about your book by a friend. After reading it I was convicted by the Holy Spirit to stay and love her more like Christ instead of like me. It is possible to do that and now I have since had her read your other book Restored to Freedom and she got completely delivered and set free. Thank you for saving my marriage and life."

"I thought I was a great Christian because I attended church every Sunday and sometimes on Wednesday night and gave my 10% tithe on my gross income amount. But after reading Loving Like Christ I discovered that I previously had no idea what a real Christian was. I was very selfish before and used to take offenses all the time and get angry. I felt so convicted after reading this book and the Lord has transformed by heart to loving others the way that I should have all along. Thank you so much for listening to the Lord and helping others to do the same. God Bless!"

"My stepson has been a thorn in my side ever since I married his mother as his father divorced his mother when he was six. I literally began to hate him and could not stand all the things he did that cost me thousands of dollars. After reading Loving Like Christ I felt totally convicted and have changed to seeing him like Christ sees him: a hurting young man that desperately needs unconditional love from a godly man. Thank you so much for being obedient."

"As a pastor I had counseled many couples who got remarried and it was always the same story. One spouse did things to hurt or irritate the other spouse and stepchildren did not get along with their step parent. After reading Loving Like Christ I see how we are really supposed to love and now recommend your book to all my clients that I see. Very few understand why we are called to love like Christ and then how to actually do it and what the benefits are when we allow ourselves to endure hurting people."

Acknowledgements

I want to thank my good friend Robia Scott who helped support me through an extremely challenging time in my life enduring horrific attacks from the enemy trying to steal, kill and destroy me. You were the only person in the world that knew what I was going through during the tumultuous storms and through the Lord's wisdom and discernment helped me survive and ultimately escape to the other side. Without you my ministry would have been shut down by the enemy and the lives of thousands around the world would never have been impacted and freed in Christ. Thank you.

I also want to thank Chris Schuman for his meticulous editing of my book that will ultimately change the lives of a generation of people from anger and pain into one of love and forgiveness. You are an extremely detailed and diligent man with an eye for perfection and I am honored to call you my brother.

I want to especially thank all of my family and friends that the Lord has brought into my life who truly love me unconditionally and know my heart to help people with all I am capable of through Christ. You are all awesome and I love you for your support and dedication:

(Aggie, April, Ashley, Austin, Becca, Bill, Bob, Brandon, Brian, C, Carrie, Cassandra, Cassia, Cindy, Charles, Chris, Chuck, David, Dawn, Deborah, Duane, Elaine, Erin, Garry, George, Gina, Hannah, Keith, James, Jan, Jana, Jess, Jessica, Joe, John, Jordan, Judy, Julie, Kaleigh, Larry, Luke, Marshall, Marvin, Megan, Michael, Michelle, Misty, Neil, Nick, Nova, Owen, Patti, Patty, Paul, Phil, Priscilla, Randy, Remon, Robia, Ron, Steve, Sue, Taylor, Todd, Trond, Tyler, and Tim)

Table of Contents

Foreword   Robia Scott   15

Introduction   18

Chapter 1 Life Begins   22

Chapter 2 Decisions, Decisions   30

Chapter 3 Growing Pains   43

Chapter 4 The Covenant of Marriage   51

Chapter 5 Step by Step   63

Chapter 6 What does the Bible say?   71

Chapter 7 What Did Moses Do?   89

Chapter 8 What Did Hosea Do?   96

Chapter 9 What Did Jesus Do?   101

Chapter 10 What Did Paul Do?   108

Chapter 11 Can Christians Have Demons?   113

Chapter 12 How to Love Like Christ   122

References   130

Foreword

The message of love is the message. It seems that everywhere I turn as of late, teachers, preachers and ministers of the gospel that have ears to hear what the Spirit is saying, are hearing the same thing: it is all about love! But truthfully, love is a word that is always in season because it is the foundation of Christianity. "Walking in love" is a term we sometimes throw around as believers, but love, agape love, the God kind of love, is far from a casual catchphrase.

I personally grew up incredibly influenced by the media regarding love. Mainstream music, television, and film convinced me that love was based primarily on passionate feelings and to act according to how I felt. Not only was I persuaded by the entertainment industry, but I also spent twenty years of my life smack dab in the middle of it as a professional dancer touring the world with musicians such as Prince, and then starring in various films and television shows like Buffy the Vampire Slayer.

It wasn't until I became a Christian in my late 20's that I began to learn what real, biblical love is. The God kind of love is what we think, say, and do when we are not having loving thoughts or feelings. It is a not a mere word or a feeling but a choice!

"My little children, let us not love in word or in tongue, but in deed and in truth."

1 John 3:18

True love is how we treat those that are the most difficult to love, and that is exactly what Nelson Schuman addresses in *Loving like Christ – How to Love the Hard to Love People in your Life*. As scripture teaches us in the book of Luke chapter 6 verses 27-36, loving those who love us is easy. Everyone can do that, even ungodly people, but loving those that persecute us, use us, and mistreat us, loving hard to love people, that is the real challenge. *Loving like Christ – How to Love the Hard to Love People in your Life*, is a call to maturity. It is a book for every believer that desires to abide in the fruit of the Spirit.

In the years that I have known Nelson he continually exemplifies a true love walk. He has a sincere and fiery love for God and people. He not only talks the talk, but he walks the walk, and he has a passion and a call from God to help others do the same. When it comes to the message of this book, Nelson writes in a way that, quite simply, makes it simple. His style is down to earth, and he offers multiple, real life examples of how to love and live in freedom.

16

If you long to know the heart of Christ, then this book is definitely for you.

~Robia Scott

Author - *Counterfeit Comforts*

Introduction

We are all called to love like Christ loved, but what does that really look like on a day to day basis? When you wake up in the morning and your spouse first speaks a word out to you that is not loving - how do you react? When your son or daughter talks back to you in disrespect - how does that feel and what do you say back to them in response? When you are at work and a co-worker puts you down for the hard work that you just completed and tries to make you look bad to others including your manager - what is your response? When you drive home from work and someone cuts you off in traffic and does not wave to you in requesting forgiveness - how does it make you feel and do you respond in anger back to them? What do you do if someone at your church spreads a false rumor about you to the pastor and other leaders that hurts you to your core – what do you say to them and others that believe it? Do you take an offense against them and let anger rise up in you and drive you to take revenge personally against them for the pain that they caused you? Or do you give them to God and let Him make it right in the best way for His Kingdom which may take weeks, months or even years to see right come from the wrong?

Unfortunately there are millions and millions of hurting people in this world that hurt others with their words and actions on an everyday basis and most people (including most Christians) take the bait from the enemy and become offended and then retaliate with words and actions that are not what Christ commanded us to do. Instead of turning the other cheek they try to hurt them back as harshly as they were hurt – and then either a breakdown in the relationship occurs or feelings of anger and hatred develop; ultimately hurting the person who was initially offended. Does this sound familiar to you? In reality I have seen this happen every day. The enemy laughs at all the people from whom he has been able to steal peace; causing people to be angry with each other and blame each other, robbing them of the joy that the Lord has for them.

So how does one actually love all people like Christ called us to do? How do we put aside our "right" to be offended and become unable to be offended and see them through the eyes of Christ as a hurting child that was hurt by their father or mother growing up or never knew their parents at all and had to learn to stand on their own because they never experienced trust and unconditional love from their parents; thus producing an adult with deep hurts that have never been processed nor healed by Jesus. So if a person never experienced love from parents that they could trust then how would you expect to receive love from them? One cannot give what they never received nor have inside of them. What percent of people in this world grew up with both parents that loved them the way the Lord intended? I would say less than 25%. This explains why this world is full of hurting people who have experienced traumas that have hurt their hearts and have never recovered to stand on their own and exhibit the feelings of love, joy and peace.

A boy grows up without his father because his father divorced his mother because she was too controlling and manipulative over him causing him to leave her in order to live in peace. She was too controlling because her father rejected her and controlled her telling her what to do and manipulating her free will in order to receive his approval and earn conditional love. He did this because he grew up never knowing his father because he was working all the time and not available for him to talk with thus he seemed like a bother and never bonded in the true unconditional love he deserved. So the dysfunction becomes a generational curse that goes on and on and on until someone finally recognizes it and says "I do not want to live this way anymore" and cries out to Jesus to heal their hurting heart and chooses to forgive their father or mother from all the wounds that they took from them in their life.

So what do those of us do who the Lord has put in relationship with those hard to love people who have been hurt by others? Do we take offense at their behavior and harass them back and engage in strife and verbal fights and then ultimately leave them or "disown" them? Do we tell them how messed up they are and verbally get in their face and demand that they stop behaving horribly, causing more strife, arguments, anger and hatred? What does the Lord say about this? What if you were put in a position to deal with an extreme situation of dysfunction because the Lord knew that you were more than capable to endure the trial and would help change someone's life from extreme pain, fear and anger into a life of peace and love; helping them to reach their destiny in what the Lord has for them? Sometimes we are called by the Lord to be in relationship with others that cause us to experience great suffering by sacrificing our own peace in order to help a hurting and devastated person get to the other side and escape beyond their past. If you do not endure to the end they may never change and get healed and ultimately get to heaven. Also, when you go through this extreme ordeal willingly and do not complain throughout the entire process, you will also change and become even more like Christ as your ability to be patient and suffer long will grow and your discernment to see who a person can become in Christ will develop more sharply as you see them the way God sees them. Is it an easy process to endure tremendous suffering for another person willingly? Absolutely not! But you can do it as the Lord is counting on you! If not you…then who? Lord, send me!

<u>Chapter 1</u>

Life Begins

Life begins at conception and develops in the mother's womb for nine months before the baby arrives into the world. Many parents are excited about getting pregnant with the anticipation of a new child being brought into the world; looking forward to raising them up into a young boy or girl in the nurture and admonition of the Lord. They also look forward to loving and enjoying their new child and getting to know their little personalities as they develop. They are excited about seeing them grow up, having fun with them, watching how they become their own person and how they develop their own personal relationship with the Lord. However, some parents are not at all happy about learning that they will soon see a child enter into the world. They become worried at the point they realize that they now have the responsibility of a new life on the way and are not looking forward to a child being born due to several factors such as: they were not planning to have any children for another year or two, they have limited funds so cannot afford a child comfortably and are worried they will have to live a poorer more frugal lifestyle, or perhaps they had just given birth to a child a few months before or the parents were not married and so the child will grow up without an intact and loving, cohesive family structure. The enemy tries to hurt a child as soon as he possibly can in order to steal, kill and destroy the destiny that the Lord has for them. The majority of children that are born today do not grow up in a loving and peaceful environment with both parents living healthy Christian lives and sharing the same values that are spoken of in the Bible. Therefore they are behind the eight ball from the very beginning and much pain and anguish are waiting for them to receive once they arrive.

So let's paint a scenario of a typical home environment that many children grow up in today all over the world. Many do not have both parents intact and are not stable financially due to one or both of their parents being hurt in their lives by their parents or others in relationship with them in life. So the child grows up with the lack of unconditional love from one or both parents and often times they receive harsh words spoken over them that causes them pain which just beats them down over and over throughout their youth. So as they grow up they have been hurt thousands of times from their parents as well as from those that they have gone to school with (children can be extremely cruel to their classmates) and thus they feel constantly drained of all emotionally healthy love and are full of sadness and depression. Those people in their lives have given up on them and spoken harsh words constantly so that they have no sense of value in their lives. Thus, all the negative words and actions that they have received over their short lives have produced tremendous pain, anguish and anger. Then they take out that pain on all those that cross paths with them. Thus, everyone that interacts with a person who has been hurt severely in their life receives the brunt of that pain and most of those people then try to avoid being around them because it only brings them down and hurts them to endure being in their presence.

So it becomes a vicious cycle that continues from one generation to another. Hurting people hurt people and those that have tried to love them tend to give up after a few encounters or in some cases several years of a miserable relationship as they do not see improvements quickly enough and are told by the enemy and this world that they deserve better and should have a life full of joy and fun thus leaving them to live in their pain and misery. Every time they are around the hurting person they feel like life is being drained from them and they are not strong enough in the Lord to withstand.

How many people do you know in your life that you enjoy being around who speak negative and depressing words from their mouths the majority of the time? It is very hard to stay positive when you are around them - to say the least. When you say something positive to them it is like being around Eeyore from Winnie the Pooh. "Lovely day isn't it?" is responded with "If it is a good day, which I doubt." So it becomes easier to commiserate with them and before you know it you have changed to look at the dark side of things so that you can have a conversation with them because they are so depressed and incapable of looking at the bright side of things. Then you become sad, despondent and hopeless and now you are both in the same leaking boat drowning in your sorrow!

Many people that have been hurt are also very worried and anxious about everything that could possibly go wrong in their loved ones' lives or their own. Have you ever been around a person who is filled with tremendous anxiety and fear? You can literally feel the anxiety as it envelops you when you are in the same room with them and typically causes you to lose your peace and become anxious if you are not careful. Everything in you wants to run away from them in order to feel at peace again and when you are not able to "get out of Dodge" you feel trapped and adrenaline fills your body telling

24

you to run. They are truly a tormented soul that constantly feels anxiety in their lives and full of fear and my compassion cries for them.

When people grow up under extremely toxic situations they become a toxic person until their hearts are healed from all their memories of pain, and unfortunately most never get healed which is very sad for them and their family. I have seen entire families who are living lives in fear, anger, anxiety, control and manipulation and everyone has physical sickness and diseases of every type and they all hate each other and others outside of their own family. It is such a sad state of affairs and I have extreme sympathy for anyone that has to live in such noxiousness because there is never a moment of peace or unconditional love. It brings tears to my eyes and the Lord grieves for those that have to endure this constant nightmare that never ends. Some of these families live in such despair that they feel the only way out is to take their own lives. The enemy whispers to them in their minds over and over trying to get them to check out of life early. The battlefield of the mind with the enemy is a very real thing.

So what does one do that marries into this dysfunction? Many separate or divorce wanting to be able to live in a more peaceful environment because they are not strong in the Lord themselves and do not want to sacrifice their life for another. But what if God has called you to be the answer to all this insanity? What if the Lord trusted that you could be proven faithful to being Christ to the hurting family members and that if you endure one, five, ten or more years that you could finally help your loved one(s) change forevermore? You will be surprised at what you are capable of enduring and ultimately how, when you trust in the Lord, He will be faithful and just to complete the work that He started through you in them. He honors those of His people who have willingly sacrificed their own lives for another and will ultimately bless you greatly with the respect that you are due and in many other ways of which you have no idea. So even though in your own human strength you could never put up with someone taking advantage of you and treating you horribly, using you, verbally berating you constantly, and even physically coming against you; when you are transformed through the spirit of Christ then you can do it. Philippians 4:13 NKJV, "I can do all things through Christ who strengthens me."

It may feel like you cannot stand going through another verbal barrage from your spouse, child or other family member every day, year after year....but you can do it. Think of it like you are taking one for the team – except the team is for God and His people that have been hurt in severe ways. God will reward you for your faithfulness. Is it hard to go through suffering willingly due to another person's taking their pain out on you? Yes. Unequivocally the answer is absolutely yes. But it will be worth it in the end. Too many people talk to other people and ask for opinions instead of going to the Lord to see what He wants. Most people tell them to not tolerate anything and they need boundaries (which is true to some extent, although when you are dealing with people that have enemy spirits it is of little help). Then they check out early and take the easy way out and leave the relationship instead of seeing a miracle transformation.

There were some pastors at a church that actually counseled a woman to divorce her husband based on her lies to them about him when she was the one that actually abused her husband in extreme ways for their entire marriage. He had finally separated from her as the Lord directed him - after six years hoping to get her to change to be nice and tolerable. The senior pastor of the church refused to talk to the husband because he had already made up his mind based on the lies of the husband's wife. Instead of going to the Lord and asking Him to explain the truth of the matter - the pastor kicked the innocent man out of his church and then eventually brought a curse upon his own church and lost most of his congregation as people could sense ungodly things that were occurring as well as false teaching that was being proclaimed from the pulpit. The man

26

forgave the pastors at the church and his wife but the Lord held them all accountable for what they had done and dealt with their sinful collaboration. So it is so very important to press in to the Lord for the truth and insight instead of talking to other people because unfortunately they can lie.

So what would God say to you? As long as your life is not in immediate danger from knife or glass throwing, physical assaults, and other potentially hazardous demonic behavior – I believe He would say to set an example for your spouse or children so they can see Christ in you. How many times did Jesus say we should forgive? Matt. 18:21-22 NKJV, "[21] Then Peter came to Him and said, "Lord, how often shall my brother sin against me, and I forgive him? Up to seven times?" [22] Jesus said to him, "I do not say to you, up to seven times, but up to seventy times seven." So did that mean we only have to forgive them 490 times and then we can stop?

To fully comprehend what Jesus was saying, we need to look at the context of the whole chapter. Jesus was speaking not only about forgiving one another but about Christian character, both inside and out of the church. The admonition to forgive our brother seventy times seven follows Jesus' sermon on discipline in the church (Matthew 18:15-20) in which He lays down the rules for restoring a brother who sins. Peter, wishing to appear especially forgiving, asked Jesus if forgiveness was to be offered seven times. The Jewish rabbis at the time taught that forgiving someone more than three times was unnecessary, citing Amos 1:3-13 where God forgave Israel's enemies three times, then punished them. By offering forgiveness more than double that of the Old Testament example, perhaps Peter was expecting an extra pat on the back from Jesus. When Jesus responded with 490 times, far beyond that which Peter was proposing, it probably shocked the disciples. Although they had been around Jesus for some time, they were still thinking in the limited terms of the law, instead of the unlimited terms of grace.

So by saying that we are to forgive those who sin against us seventy times seven, Jesus was not limiting forgiveness to 490 times, a number that is, for all practical purposes, beyond counting and of keeping track. Christians with forgiving hearts not only do not limit the number of times they forgive; they continue to forgive with as much grace the thousandth time as they do the first time. Christians are only capable of this type of forgiving spirit because the Spirit of God lives within us, and it is He who provides the ability to offer forgiveness over and over, just as God forgives us over and over.

Jesus' parable of the unforgiving servant comes directly after His "seventy times seven" speech, driving home the point that if we are forgiven the enormous debt of sin against a holy God, then how much more should we be eager to forgive those who sin against us, who are just as sinful as they? Paul equates this example in Ephesians 4:32 where he admonishes us to forgive one another "even as God for Christ's sake has forgiven you." So we should forgive everyone for everything and anything that anyone ever does to cause us to be hurt. If all Christians took this stance there would rarely be divorce in the church and the enemy could not cause division within churches, families and work environments.

Forgiveness is such an amazingly healthy thing to do for someone that hurts us. It is similar to grace in that the person does not deserve it but as Christians we are required to give it or else a root of bitterness will be able to spring up inside of us. The challenge comes in when a person is not repentant. Then do we still forgive them or hold it over them. I have known many people who will not forgive and then it literally eats them alive. They develop sickness and diseases that cause them to have so much pain that they are living in hospitals and doctors' offices. Once a person chooses not to forgive they unfortunately invite the enemy to come into their lives and hurt them because it gives the enemy a right to harm them as they opened a door for the enemy to enter.

No, it is not for the faint of heart and few can actually willingly walk in the shoes of Christ but it can be done and should be done to truly be a Christian as the Lord called us to do. We must never take any offenses from anyone because it gives the enemy the right to hurt us. Clearly, forgiveness is not to be given out in a limited fashion but is to be abundant and available to all, just as the limitless grace of God is poured out upon us. So forgive freely to everyone and often.

Chapter 2

Decisions, Decisions

I always found it very interesting to think about how you could have two people raised in the same family under the same father and mother yet one is living solidly for the Lord while the other is living for the world and having major trauma affect them all of their days. It all comes down to what decisions were made by each of the siblings throughout their lifetimes. Those decisions that aligned with the Lord would be blessed and receive favor and protection as well as bring them peace while the one that chose the world's ways would receive curses, sickness, strife and more emotional pain. Just saying "No" to attending a party with alcohol being served when you were sixteen years old versus saying yes could avoid some very bad circumstances from occurring in your life (car accidents, probation, kicked off sporting teams in high school, etc). Or at the same age? saying "No" to having sex with a person you are not married to instead of saying "Yes" and later becoming pregnant, changing your life forever with added expenses but no income for which to provide, changes in options for advanced education, being disowned by parents for hurting their reputation, etc. All these things can happen because the enemy whispers in your mind to follow the desires of your flesh instead of the purity of the Lord. Much is fear-based which drives us to not trust in the Lord nor others that are healthy and good.

The enemy tries to influence everyone in the world to make decisions that are ungodly to try and steal, kill and destroy us. He does so by whispering to you in your mind and 90% of what you hear sounds good, yet there is always a "gotcha" that leads you away from the decision that is ultimately best for you. He will normally go after you with a fleshly desire that will feed off of your need for affirmation and feeling loved. He will also appeal to your pride in making decisions or how you will look to others in your family, church or ministry. So if you are a young lady who never received the unconditional love that you deserved from your father, then the enemy will tempt you to be drawn to a boy or young man to receive it but unfortunately the young man will be drawn to you to receive a short term sexual release that could produce a baby that the enemy could then cause you to make a decision to abort causing even more feelings of guilt and condemnation your entire life. So you can see just how the enemy works in your life – and just because you give your life to the Lord the enemy does not just stop speaking to you. Christians are affected by demonic voices all the time until they become closer to the Lord and know who they are in Christ and then can discern the voice of the enemy versus the Lord as well as be completely delivered from demons that have a right to co-exist within them due to either sin they committed or was done to them or was a generational curse from someone up their family line.

It is so important to realize that just one bad decision that the enemy tempts you to act on can alter your life and cause years of pain that if never resolved will cause not only emotional difficulties but even physical sickness and disease for a lifetime. The enemy is real and does speak to you whether you realize it or not. You will hear one of three voices in your mind – the enemy, your own and the Lord's or Holy Spirit. So to live the life that the Lord wants for you it is imperative to discern when the enemy is talking to you and when the Lord or Holy Spirit is. Get to know the difference as early as you can in your life. How can you know the difference between the enemy and the Lord?

The enemy's voice sounds just like your own thoughts but if you think ahead to the possible ramifications to choosing his decisions you will always see it takes you farther away from the Lord and usually provides temporary or short term fleshly pleasures. Sex, drugs, alcohol and food are all imitations of what we are looking to satisfy in our desire to be loved unconditionally. Sex with your spouse is good while sex with someone we are not married to creates a covenant with them that needs to be broken off and severed because it can create myriad relational issues the rest of your life. Drugs cause a temporary high feeling to your system but later you crash down and feel empty and guilty and need to strive towards your next high and never receive the critical peace that you are looking for over and over again. Ultimately the spirits that have a right to you when you do the drugs (spirits of Pharmakeya) will whisper to you words of discouragement, condemnation and even worthlessness and suicide. Alcohol also is used to get us temporarily unfocused off of our tremendous pain inside our hearts to escape for as long as possible. But you can never escape that empty void with this counterfeit diversion and can actually cause far greater damage to all your relationships as the spirit of alcohol develops more words from the enemy and causes you to have feelings of depression and suicide. Then there is the desire to eat food to escape our failures and pain which only leads to gaining weight and obesity or the opposite by binging and purging. Only freedom in Christ can overcome the enemy's temptations in life.

So how does a person who has been hurt over and over again by their father, mother and others in life make good life decisions every day? When the enemy is whispering to them and they are not recognizing that it is the enemy speaking to them it is extremely hard as they feel like they are being tossed to and fro in the wind like a boat in the ocean with no rudder. I have seen one woman who was so tormented by the enemy's voice that she could not make a simple decision as to what to order for lunch at a restaurant without asking multiple questions of their server; exasperating all those waiting to get their orders placed having to wait ten minutes while she decided if she felt like eating fish, chicken or steak and then how to prepare it and what sides and kind of water to drink. Her father used to verbally berate her if she or her siblings made any decisions that he did not agree with. Thus she was programmed to try to never make a wrong decision in her life even when trying to make very simple ones such as what to eat or how to drive from one place to another as she always had to find the shortest distance or fastest pace (thank God for GPS now).

One young man could not stop having sex with girls because he was in so much pain from losing a relationship with a girl that he cared for deeply for many years. He so desperately wanted loved but knew that it was not satisfying his broken heart. This went on for years. A couple of the young women became pregnant as he could not stop the behavior that he knew was wrong, but the enemy spirits in him kept telling him that sex would give him love; but he never felt loved because it was void of the true godly love that he needed.

The ability to make the right decisions is clouded by the presence of the enemy in their lives and until they recognize that they are being influenced by the enemy and command the spirits to go, then they will continue to make bad decisions that are not aligned with the Lord. Once the spirits are commanded to go from them then the person will only need to deal with any remaining negative mindsets that have been on them for many years, and thus the process of improvement and change begins.

One young man was hurt by a boy a year older than him when he was eight and was driven by those spirits that entered him to do a lot of destructive behaviors. He provoked his younger brother and sister causing strife constantly. He would not listen to his father or mother and coaches and other authority figures. He was placed in Christian counseling, but they did not know how to deliver the spirits from him and just diagnosed him with ADHD and medicated him which caused him to lose his appetite; and he was already skinny. He began to get more physically abusive when he became a teenager and even punched his father twice in the chin during one intense exchange. His father had a tough decision to make – should he press charges or not. He chose not to after agonizing over it and then considered moving him out of their home to a home for troubled youth, but no place would take him. The boy decided one day that it would be wise to put these plastic circles in his ear lobes called gauges. Unfortunately he kept deciding to make the gauges larger until one day it got so big that it actually tore his earlobe and so he had a dangling earlobe for several weeks before his employer told him to get it fixed because it was grossing out the customers. That decision later cost him $700 for one earlobe to be fixed by a plastic surgeon. Then eventually he started to be promoted into management so had to fix the other earlobe which cost him another $700. Each of our decisions has a future impact whether we realize it or not. When the enemy is driving our decision making process it never turns out well.

Then one day his father was taught about praying more effectively with the authority of Jesus Christ. He was told that when we pray the way Jesus taught, then we would see miracles happen. When we pray the way the rest of the world prays – pleading with God to do something – unfortunately nothing usually happens. So one day he decided to give it a try after his son was once again making wrong decisions and he asked him if he could pray for him.

34

To his shock his son actually agreed to allow him to pray. So he gently commanded the spirits to go from him and instantly the demonic spirits left him and never returned. But while the spirits instantly left him he still had mindsets that were in place which caused him to continue to speak out in foul language at times and have some outward behaviors that were not of the Lord. The constant torment of making bad decisions to hurt himself, however, was removed as he could now think more clearly without the undue presence of the spirits affecting him. He was able to finally reason and make much wiser decisions that were good and healthy for him and ended up being calmer and never having any physical outbursts ever again.

When his father was enduring the ten years of hell of parenting him - being affected by his son's selfish and hurtful decisions - he never saw him as God saw him. He saw him as a tremendous "thorn in his side" who made his life a living hell every day and who was a constant pain full of strife with no peace. He was so desperate to live in a life of peace instead of daily torment and violence year after year. When the father finally was told by an anointed man who began to mentor him that his son was really a very sweet, kind and gentle soul who was a lot like him – then he began to change and see him from a different perspective. It was like a revelation to his spirit as he now could see him as he was going to be and not who he behaved liked for the past ten years. He developed a tremendous compassion for him as he knew he was truly in torment as the spirits spoke to him and caused him to do things that were not who he really was. It was very hard to see him the way God saw him before because he had behaved so horribly for so long and he was constantly in strife with his father, mother and siblings. Once he could see him in the spirit as a young man that was like him, then he could visualize the transformation beginning.

The Lord told one man that he would love his wife like Christ loved the church a few months before he married her. Then once he married her he discovered a side of her that was very controlling, manipulative and deceitful; and then the Lord told him that he was not allowed to tell a human soul what he was going to endure until the Lord released him and one day his wife would speak about it all over the world and give him the proper honor that he deserved. The Lord never told him how long the season would last as he just had to trust the Lord. So he endured extreme constant verbal abuse as it was like Satan himself was speaking through her to him every day and night as he worked from his home and she did not work for several years. He also suffered several physical assaults and even some sexual abuse. He kept it all a secret from all that knew them including all the church and ministry people that they interacted with - covering up her thousands of offenses along the way as she threatened him not to ever tell anyone. Finally after more than six years later of suffering in silence in extreme ways, the Lord called him to separate from her and that He would bless him greatly in ministry while the Lord would finish what he had started in her healing process and bring her to the end. It was a true act of self-sacrifice in every way imaginable and one that would pay dividends for countless people around the world in order to help them get freed from similar torment of powerful spirits attacking them called the Jezebel and Leviathan spirits which are explained in detail in my book *Restored to Freedom*.

When we see someone the way God sees them it changes us to have much more compassion and patience than we otherwise would. People that choose to make their own lives miserable by making bad decisions are only doing so out of their pain. Who wants to make their own life total misery every day, month, year and sometimes a lifetime? The enemy wants to steal, kill and destroy our peace and life. When the Lord brings us into the lives of those who are behaving in pain, we often times have to sacrifice what we know to be the best decision for them to make in order to allow them to make a bad decision. They are not capable of listening to our wisdom and advice yet and it will create tremendous strife between us. In some cases their decision may cost us thousands or tens of thousands of dollars, causing us to potentially be impacted financially in a major way.

One man married a woman whose sons were greatly hurt by her previous three failed marriages. The Lord called him to marry her to show her and her sons what a real man of God was like as they had not known any like him before. The elder son made various poor decisions and needed some help on other bills that cost his new step father over fifty-thousand dollars in six years. His younger brother also needed help from his stepfather to allow him to live in a home by paying a greatly reduced rent and to not have to pay utilities for several years. One year he lost his job and the stepson could not afford to pay any of his rent or utilities to him. Thus after six years the stepfather had to pay over $85,000 for both stepsons' needs. Was it worth it? From a financial perspective to the step-father it would look like it was the worst decision he could have made for himself personally, but both sons learned what a real man of God does for those he loves and for the first time they had faith in a man who would willingly lay down his life for their betterment. It began to slowly change the sons to choosing to live lives more like their stepfather and become more responsible and to help give more of themselves to others who were hurting. It caused them to have hope - that if this man would sacrifice for them so greatly that perhaps they should also change and become more like Christ. So eternally it was exactly the right decision to make as a stepfather. Would many men do this today? Probably not – perhaps no one as it cost the stepfather all that he had and he had to go into great debt for them. But the Lord instructed him to do it and he did and then the Lord provided for the man and ultimately years later rewarded him greatly for his extreme act of obedience and sacrifice with a powerful ministry helping countless lives to freedom from the enemy.

When we see others through the compassion of Christ we realize why the bad decisions are being made by so many people and we have more patience, long suffering and love which help us to understand them instead of judging and berating the person for the bad choices they have made. "Love them like Jesus" is a song by Casting Crowns that was released in 2005 that is very powerful and I encourage you to watch the video. It talks about various people's everyday life pains that many experience and how we should have compassion in our reactions to those that have been hurt through them (failed marriages, children that die early, etc). Some of the lyrics are as follows:

Casting Crowns "Love them like Jesus"

"The love of her life is drifting away

They're losing the fight for another day

The life that she's known is falling apart

A fatherless home, a child's broken heart

You're holding her hand, you're straining for words

You're trying to make – sense of it all

She's desperate for hope, darkness clouding her view

She's looking to you

Just love her like Jesus, carry her to Him

His yoke is easy, His burden is light

You don't need the answers to all of life's questions

Just know that He loves her and stay by her side

Love her like Jesus

Love her like Jesus"

I used to not have any compassion for people that had gone through a divorce because I never experienced it until after 17 years of my first marriage. But once I had to actually go through a divorce I could now relate in a very real way to the extreme hurt that I felt when I could not stop it. I saw my children getting hurt through it and I could not help them from the resulting negative behavior that ensued. It was horrible in every aspect because I knew that divorce was not of the Lord and those that do it are either being affected by the enemy or their spouse is. The enemy is always behind every divorce by causing either one spouse to cause great hurt and pain to their mate, or the other spouse is having the enemy on them telling them to leave their loved one. If I had never gone through that trauma I would not have the extreme compassion that I now have for others that have endured a divorce. I see them like Jesus does and now counsel many, many couples who have been on the verge of divorce and have seen most all completely set free from the enemy and saved their marriages and know how beautiful that is to the Lord and to the couple and their children. There is something about walking in the shoes of others that becomes a true life experience that no book training can do for you to replicate. When you have actually experienced loving someone that was hard to love and allowed yourself to be yelled at or cursed at while at the same time realizing that was not really who the person is but rather who they are in the pain that they have experienced - then it causes you to be able to withstand the battle at hand and ultimately change into being more like Christ.

Jesus loves us no matter what we have done and we are called to love others in the same way as we are Christ's ambassadors and through us others can feel the love they never received from those they should have. So while living with someone who makes decisions that are not wise and that actually cost us money we may not be able to afford is not at all fun or easy, if you can realize that you are there to be a Christ-like figure to them, then you are better able to endure it to the end. The end being the person's life changing from one of the enemy to one of your friend and living a life of a true Christian. Remember the "What Would Jesus Do?" bracelets that were the craze back in the 1990's? Think about that every time someone does something that causes you pain or when you feel like taking an offense over something done to you. Would Jesus ever pay them back for what they did? Would he EVER get into verbal strife with them? I do not think so. However, I have thought about the issue of being married to someone that gets in your face and verbally assaults you for hours every day. Since Jesus was never married he never had to endure that – so what would He do if he was? I know that He might have cast out the demon that was affecting his spouse to get her freed since He really knew His authority - but what about in the cases of free will in his spouse? If the spouse really wanted to keep an unclean spirit in them such as the Jezebel spirit, then they could - even though it would hurt them in the long run.

So what do you do if your spouse is afflicted with the Jezebel spirit - which can only be cast out by them and not you by recognizing that they have it and are operating in it and then commanding it to go from them? That spirit is extremely hard to get free from because your spouse would need to first recognize and admit that they have it and then command it to go. Many deny that they have it and would rather stay in control and divorce their spouse then admit they have it and command the spirit to go. My book *Restored to Freedom* is very revelatory and effective in explaining how a person gets the Jezebel spirit and then how to command it to go through effective renunciation prayers and has seen tremendous success in saving marriages around the world. Essentially, a person who grows up with a father that rejected them and was controlling and manipulative will often times develop the Jezebel spirit which causes them to be very controlling and manipulative to their spouse (and sometimes children) and will often times be drawn to a church or ministry looking for more position and authority as their spirit of pride is very strong. They will want to lead various ministries at

40

church and elsewhere but ultimately will attempt to shut down anyone operating in the prophetic giftings or healing ministries as they look to move themselves up to higher positions of control and power.

Living with people that are constantly striving with you is very challenging and wears you down emotionally and physically to say the least. You need to take breaks by separating from them on a regular basis by going on private walks alone or bike rides or something that brings you peace. When you are alone, talk to the Lord and ask Him to provide you with the patience to endure the trial and strength to continue on and to see the person through His eyes. If they call and text you while you are alone explain to them nicely that you need to be alone in order to spend time with them so they know that you are not planning to leave them as their previous spouses or caregivers might have done. They need to be reassured that you love them and they can trust you. One thing that may help is if you can tell the person that is hurting you calmly that when they are behaving controlling or being mean to you that it really hurts your heart and causes you to not want to be around them. When they hear that they are hurting you over and over they will sometimes start to change and take some ownership in the strife and realize what they are doing but sometimes they will still show no remorse and will continue to try to dominate you in every way imaginable.

Showing grace and love to someone who has made your life challenging is what we as Christians are called to do. Grace does not stop after they have hurt you one hundred times or one hundred thousand. It keeps on giving and giving and never gives up. While it may seem like the person will never change and the enemy will definitely whisper in your ear that you are a fool for allowing them to continue hurting you – the Lord will reward you for your faithfulness and not giving up.

So while people who have been hurt make many poor decisions that make their lives and yours worse – you can still show them love and compassion like Christ by seeing them through the

41

eyes of Christ. While you must modify your reactions to them and be extremely forgiving and patient – it is possible to love them the way God has called us. Love them like Jesus.

Chapter 3

Growing Pains

When people come to the Lord for the first time and receive Jesus as their savior what happens to them? Their hearts should start to change from a desire to serve themselves and feed their fleshly desires to wanting to serve the Lord and mature in their spirit. But everyone changes on different timelines and with different personalities based on how they grew up, what their desires are in the Lord, what their calling is in life, who they may marry and who they have as children or stepchildren. Perhaps you grew up and your father was busy working all the time and never knew the Lord and your mother was not involved in spiritual things because she had an abusive father and so she did not show much love to you at all. Then let's say that you gave your life to the Lord when you were at a church camp as a teenager but when you came home and told your parents they were not interested so they could not share in your excitement and passion. The results of that non-reaction hurt you and caused you to learn that you could not trust them to protect your heart and your desires so you had to keep things to yourself in order to not get hurt again; although you were desperate for any small bit of love that they might decide to give you conditionally from time to time as life went on. As long as you did exactly what they wanted they would like you, but if you made any decisions that they did not agree with then they would threaten to disown you in order to manipulate you to do exactly what they wanted.

Then as you matured in age your brother contracts a rare disease and dies and most of your family loses their faith in God and can only trust in themselves to survive. Therefore you do not really know God nor can you trust Him even though in your head you know you are supposed to totally trust in Him because every Christian tells you that is how it works. So you become a Christian in name only without being able to trust Him to meet all your needs. Your father says he is a Christian but overly controls his family and hurts his children with his harsh words and judgments and rejects them when he does not want to see them. Your mom feels so sad due to the loss of her son that she barely recognizes you as her daughter.

Then you end up marrying the first man who comes into your life. He says he is a Christian so that you will love him, but once married you find that he has no desire for anything godly. After a few years he desires to leave you due to your controlling ways that you developed from not having a genuinely loving father. After he divorces you, the pain of tremendous rejection from another man further develops an anger inside of you for all men and you make a vow that "I will never submit to any man!" yet you desire to be married so you try it again. This time you try to control your new husband, but he divorces you after a couple of years. Now you really do not trust a man and say that all men cannot be trusted. Each time that you marry a man and the relationship fails your heart gets more broken and you get more angry and want to hurt more men to get back at them for the pain that they caused you.

You attend church and have a desire to grow closer to God but you have no concept of who God really is and how He loves you unconditionally because of your experiences with men. You develop a strong fear because you do not really know the Lord although those at church think you love the Lord because they are not discerning in the spirit and you put on a good show in front of them. So then you marry a third man and think you hit it big because he works for a very large worldwide ministry which will help you gain a position of importance in the ministry due to your association with your husband. Unfortunately you are so fractured in your thinking due to all the previous men that left you that you try controlling him even more and then he eventually separates and leaves you shortly after a year. So now you are in your late 40's and time is running out on you ever living in a peaceful situation with a man and doing any ministry and you feel ashamed of what you are becoming yet always blame the other men instead of looking at yourself.

When you go to your various counselors throughout your life you do not tell all of the truth so they cannot help you with all the pain you have in your heart and anger for the men that rejected you - which started with your father. Your walk with the Lord is really no closer than it was before but you appear to your friends like you know something because you are good at acting when in reality it is all a show based in false pretense.

So finally you try marriage one more time and this time you hit a homerun with a godly man of honor who loves you like Christ loved the church. Yet immediately you are trying to control his every move and manipulate him and are extremely anxious and even though you are desperate for love and he truly loves you – you treat him even more harshly than the first three husbands and you become emotionally, physically and sexually abusive. You have a desire to do ministry because that is who you really are in Christ but you are unable to due to the unrighteous behavior you exhibit because of your pain and anger toward men and desire to dominate them. So ultimately your fourth husband has to separate from you due to the extreme control and coercion to shut him down from doing ministry.

So after all of this your heart is extremely broken and yet you are more defiant than ever and your hatred towards men is at an all-time high. So where is your relationship with the Lord? You know in your heart of hearts that you were the one to blame for all of your broken relationships because you could never trust in men due to a spirit of fear on you, and by your controlling actions you drove them all away from you. So, even though some in the church may think that you are a loving and giving person, they can see from the trail of blood that has followed you that there is something not right with your walk with the Lord. You are exhausted from running away from the real issues and never getting your life or ministry on track for the Lord.

So what many do is live a lifetime of lies, deceit and try to hide their true behaviors that are not godly while trying to grow stronger in the Lord every year which becomes an effort in futility. So little by little they may grow somewhat but until they get completely honest and then healed in their hearts from their past they cannot help anyone. Today they are not able to help others get free of anything because hurting people hurt people and only healthy people can heal people. It is the same concept of flying on an airplane when the flight attendants show you that if the plane loses oxygen that you must first put the oxygen mask over your own face before attempting to put it on your child. If you are not healed of all of your past pains initially, then you cannot help anyone else as much as you would like because you will project your pain and wrong advice onto them.

So how do you grow in the Lord and get healed at the same time? It is usually a process that takes time as you need to break off afflicting spirits from your past that are not from the Lord. You may hear from the enemy many times every day as you are trying to serve the Lord. Thus, he continues to tempt you to sin and cause strife with your spouse and then it becomes a tug of war going back and forth for sometimes many months or even years to be totally free. So to start the process of healing you should forgive all of those that have ever hurt you. You can say "I choose to forgive my father for all the times he put me down and was not there for me and hurt my heart." So forgiveness is a requirement in order to start to be released from your past hurts. How can you tell if you have forgiven someone that has hurt you? If they come walking into the same room as you and your heartbeat does not intensify and you do not feel like either running away or attacking them then you know that you have completely forgiven them. In many cases people that hold resentment or take offenses against another person do not even have one right to do so in the first place. Many have offended others multiple times and then when finally the other person stands up for them self and says they need to part from them for the sake of their own health – the offending person then takes an offense. Go figure!

It is really ridiculous because so many hurting people hurt others and then take offenses at the drop of a hat when those people they are verbally berating either stand up for themselves and respond to them to point out their offensive behavior or they leave them and walk away. It is like you cannot win with them no matter what you do. You either are supposed to take verbal abuse as long as they want to give it to you – or you cannot respond to correct them because then they will take an offense. So, most people want nothing to do with them anymore as they have to walk on eggshells all the time around them.

So the process of growing and maturing in the Lord is exactly that....a process. Sometimes it can take us a lifetime and sadly for many they never achieve a state of peace in their lives and continue to live in fear and strife. They are always bringing up how they were hurt by their father, mother, husband or wife for years and years. They cannot just let it go and give the offending person to God. The fact is that people are going to hurt you and if you cannot love them in spite of the offense and you choose to hold a grudge against them, then you will be the one that will be hurting yourself and no one will want to be around you anymore. People are constantly striving and taking offenses at anyone that does not give them what they want and then offending people every day and wondering why no one wants to live with them anymore. It is a battle of the spirit to see who can win out – forgiveness or offense. A true Christian can be offended and not take the offense, but it usually takes time to become like this if you have grown up taking offenses your whole life and having that behavior modeled for you by your parents or siblings.

So as you grow in the Lord you should become free from the evil spirits that have afflicted you in the past but only if you recognize that they are there (I talk about them in depth in chapter 11). So for those of us that must love the ones that have been hurt dramatically and are not fun to live around – what is our Christian responsibility? How does one absorb all the hurts of those that we love without getting hurt ourselves in the process?

The Lord gave me a picture of what it can look like. Think of a dog breed called a pit bull terrier. The image that some get is of those dogs that are involved in fighting with other dogs (some to the death). In some cases pit bulls will kill another animal or even humans if they are provoked and have been taught this way. Since they are a part of the terrier family they will go after birds, squirrels and cats as their "hunting targets." But they are really very people-friendly and act like a clown by their typical behavior. They are strong willed, obedient, loyal and like to have fun. So how does a pit bull get to the point of wanting to fight to kill another dog (like the media have shown) or kill a human? They are beaten and abused over and over until they have such an anger and hatred inside that they will go after another dog or human with the potential to kill. This is similar to what happens to a human when they are raised by parents that are hurting, so then their child gets hurt through verbal emotional wounds (and worse). Then by the time they grow into adulthood they have so many wounds that they do not know how to

48

love another human being and take out all of their anger and hatred on their spouse. So when a meek and loving spouse gets married to a controlling and angry spouse, they will have to either absorb behavior that is extremely hard to deal with or they will be hurt so much that they will feel like they cannot survive.

So as a human we are trying to get past our past and grow in the Lord, but it can be a slow process for many in order to get healed. Meanwhile they get married to another person and strife comes into play that never should have entered into their covenant had they both been healthy going into the marriage. So what does one do that is healthier who marries one that has much pain and anger? They need to love them like Christ loved the church – helping them to heal and loving on them and sacrificing like Christ did for us. This is not for the weak of heart and is definitely not a life that many willingly submit themselves to for years and years in today's society that says you should "look out for yourself" and you "deserve to be happy."

So just what does God think about marriage and someone divorcing someone? Does it make him pleased when someone divorces someone who tried loving them with all their heart and soul, giving and giving to them year after year? Will the person divorcing their mate be blessed by the Lord for ending what they promised they would keep together forever? Why would a spouse control and manipulate the one they are supposed to love? Is marriage a contract between two parties or is it a covenant between two people and the Lord? What exactly is a covenant and what does it entail? The next chapter will explain what a marriage really is and what is required. If two people recognize that they are both in it for life and that neither will take the quick way out of a hurting relationship, then both can be healed and have an amazing testimony to help others that are hurting in marriage. The recent movie called *War Room* depicted a couple that was hurting in their marriage and argued frequently as they both looked at each other as the problem instead of recognizing that the enemy was the one to blame. When the wife recognized that it was a spiritual battle and started praying for her husband, then she began to change and see changes in him as well. The next chapter explains exactly what a marriage covenant means and is helpful in learning more about the importance of recognizing exactly the significance of the covenant.

Chapter 4

The Covenant of Marriage

Many people choose to get married when they are young because they love the person that they see before them who makes them happy and brings joy to their hearts. But so many do not see all the hurts and pains in their mate until after they say "I do." Then the person no longer has to act on their best behavior since they officially have you as their partner, so they can treat you the way they really feel. Many learn on their honeymoons what the person is really like and they may be in for a shock as their spouse may turn into a very angry, controlling person that you had never seen before. So then what does one do who thought they were getting the Princess Bride but actually got Godzilla? Or thought they were marrying Prince Charming but actually received Mr. Hyde?

There is a song that was released in 2015 by Casting Crowns called "Broken Together." Below are the lyrics from the song:

What do you think about when you look at me
I know we're not the fairy tale you dreamed we'd be
You wore the veil, you walked the aisle, you took my hand
And we dove into a mystery

How I wish we could go back to simpler times
Before all our scars and all our secrets were in the light
Now on this hallowed ground, we've drawn the battle lines
Will we make it through the night?

It's going to take much more than promises this time
Only God can change our minds

Maybe you and I were never meant to be complete
Could we just be broken together
If you can bring your shattered dreams and I'll bring mine
Could healing still be spoken and save us
The only way we'll last forever is broken together

How it must have been so lonely by my side
We were building kingdoms and chasing dreams and left love behind
I'm praying God will help our broken hearts align
And we won't give up the fight

It's going to take much more than promises this time
Only God can change our minds

Maybe you and I were never meant to be complete
Could we just be broken together
If you can bring your shattered dreams and I'll bring mine
Could healing still be spoken and save us
The only way we'll last forever is broken together

Maybe you and I were never meant to be complete
Could we just be broken together
If you can bring your shattered dreams and I'll bring mine
Could healing still be spoken and save us
The only way we'll last forever is broken together

The message that Casting Crowns wanted to convey is that when you come into a marriage usually both people have come from a family situation that is less than ideal, leaving each person broken. So if we can recognize that we both are not perfect, then God can heal both people during their marriage as long as one does not choose to leave the other. If only the laws of this world would be set so that both husband and wife had to both agree on divorce instead of just one person deciding to leave, then at least they would have a fighting chance of saving their marriage and not allow the enemy to claim another victim (and multiple victims when it involves children).

Mark Lane from Bible Numbers For Life describes what the marriage covenant means. If people read this before they got married and had to sign it and adhere to it, there would be far fewer divorces in the world. Also, if they read my book *Restored to Freedom* they would understand what the top reason is for divorce and how to stop the majority of the behaviors that cause divorces (control, manipulation, deceit, sexual sins, etc.) due to paternal wounds that were suffered by one of the parties. Normally a person who suffers from controlling behavior will marry someone who they can control.

A covenant is NOT a contract (as we would usually think).

A contract is an agreement between identified parties. A contract is a transaction.

A covenant is an agreement that changes the identity of the parties. A covenant is a transformation.

53

The concept of transforming one's identity is novel to some. Western thinking has moved to the principle of inalienable human rights from birth regardless of age, gender or station in life. This has not always been the case. The foundation of Western civilization is based on Judeo-Christian beliefs as taught in the Bible. In the Bible rights and privileges are not the same for all people and vary depending on age, gender, and many other criteria. As we will see, the Bible shows it is possible to change one's identity through a covenant. As would be expected, changing one's identity changes one's rights, privileges, and station in life.

THE COVENANT OF MARRIAGE

Marriage is a covenant. The Bible says: "For this reason a man will leave his father and mother and be united with his wife and they will become one flesh." (Genesis 2:24)

The bride and the groom are considered part of their respective parents' families and under their parents' authority until they are married. In Biblical teaching when a boy grows past adolescence to manhood he is not considered by God to have left his father's household. If he physically leaves home and starts a new life, he is still part of his father's household, just farther away. He may be no longer a child or an adolescent but he is still reckoned by God to be under the authority of his father. The man can only "leave his father and mother" when he is "united with his wife."

Why is that? When a child is born to a couple – the child is the literal flesh and blood of his parents. At birth the child is washed in the blood of the mother as it passes through the birth canal. The mother is one flesh with the father – so, in effect, legally speaking the blood upon the child is reckoned as that of the father as well. God looks at the parents' blood on the child and from that moment on the child is under the protection and under the authority of the parents. The child is not owned by the parents, like a chattel or a piece of furniture, but the child is under the stewardship and guardianship of the parents.

How can that change? Again blood comes into it. In the consummation of marriage, when a man and a woman have intercourse for the first time, the hymen of the woman breaks and she sheds blood. The woman's blood applies itself to the skin of the man's flesh in the woman. God sees the blood and recognizes a covenant of marriage between the man and the woman. From that point on the covenant of the guardianship of parents is annulled and the covenant of marriage is instituted.

The man and the woman are no longer under the authority of their parents - they have changed identities and are now one flesh under God – a new person in God's eyes with a new set of rights and privileges. They continue to have a duty to honor their mother and father but not to obey them.

SIGNS OF THE COVENANT OF MARRIAGE

Across the world, marriage is recognized by signs and tokens. The signs of the covenant of marriage have ancient roots and we see similar signs in other covenants in the Bible.
Some examples of tokens of marriage:

- **The shedding of blood**: at consummation - the chief token of marriage

- **Exchanging vows**: there is understanding of the covenant and verbal consent to it

- **Physical touch**: the kiss, the touch of lips to lips; the joining of hands; the marriage bed

- **Sharing a table**: eating together is a sign of intimacy, trust, and mutual bond

- **Changing names**: traditionally the woman adopts her husband's surname

- **Changing clothes**: the woman wears a new dress for the occasion plus her betrothal jewelry

- **Displaying symbols**: rings are exchanged which are worn on a finger; head covering of the woman

- **Changing residences**: the couple move to a private room or home of their own

The transformations that occur in a marriage:

- **Changing destinies**: the couple live together for the rest of their lives

- **Changing roles**: the wife submits to her husband instead of to her father and mother; the man submits to God rather than to his father and mother; the man protects and loves his wife

- **Changing purpose**: becoming progenitors, having children: the main purpose of marriage! **Changing rights**: the authority to raise, to discipline and to teach children

- **Changing responsibilities**: leading, guiding, caring and loving the members of the family

DUTIES OF A HUSBAND AND WIFE IN CHRISTIAN MARRIAGE

Guidance is provided in the New Testament regarding the duties of a husband and a wife joined under a covenant of holy matrimony before God. This teaching is God's will for Christian marriage:

- Christian marriage is monogamous: a husband takes only one wife (1 Cor. 7:2);

- Except for prayer and mutual consent each party must permit the other to enjoy intimacy of their body, meaning to come together sexually (1 Cor. 7:5);

- The marriage bed and the sharing of intimacy between a husband and his wife is exclusive; it must not be shared with others - it is holy (Heb. 13:4);

- Wives ought to be submissive to their husbands in the same way that free men ought to obey ruling authorities in the land and slaves ought to obey their masters (1 Peter 2:13 to 3:6);

- Husbands have a duty to treat their wives respectfully and considerately (1 Peter 3:7);

- Husbands have a duty to love their wives sacrificially, as Christ loved the church, who laid down his life for her (Eph. 5:25);

- Husbands and wives give up life options open to single people – they have a duty to comfort each other (1 Cor. 7:32);

- Husbands must be concerned about the affairs of the world, how to please the wife – which means to provide for her and to protect her (1 Corinthians 7:33); The husband is the spiritual leader in the home – he is responsible to teach his wife spiritual things and to instruct her in godliness that she may glorify the Lord (Eph. 5:26-27);

- The wife is to quietly and reverently submit to the husband's authority (1 Timothy 2:11-12);

- The husband is the head of the home. It is the responsibility of the wife and the children to honor the head of the home. This means to show proper respect inside the home and in the community. (Ephesians 5:23,33);

DIVORCE AND SEPARATION

- Ought the covenant of marriage ever be broken? Jesus instructed the Jews that is not the will of God.

- "... 'Is it lawful for a man to divorce his wife?' 'What did Moses command you?' ... 'Moses permitted a man to write a certificate of divorce and send her away.' 'It was because your hearts were hard that Moses wrote you this law.' Jesus replied. 'But at the beginning of creation God made them male and female: "For this reason a man will leave his father and mother and be united to his wife and the two will become one flesh." So they are no longer two but one. Therefore **what God has joined together, let man not separate.**'" (Mark 10:2-9)

- Can the covenant of marriage be broken? In speaking to Jews under the Law, Jesus taught divorce is permissible in the case of marital unfaithfulness:

- "... anyone who divorces his wife, **except for marital unfaithfulness**, causes her to commit adultery, and anyone who marries a woman so divorced commits adultery." (Matt. 5:32)

- Marital unfaithfulness is usually interpreted to mean adultery. However, as we have seen in the previous section, the duties of a Christian husband and wife extend far beyond the minimum requirement to keep the marriage bed holy. It is more likely that unfaithfulness to the duties of marriage will occur for other reasons than adultery. When unfaithfulness occurs, reconciliation is possible through repentance and forgiveness.

- Divorce might be permissible to Jews under the Law in certain circumstances, but that does not make it permissible to Christians.

- Christian marriage is meant to be a witness of the relationship of Christ's love for the church (Ephesians 5:29-32). The Lord Jesus will never 'divorce' Christians, no matter how much we stray. His love for us is profound, and his forgiveness of our sins is everlasting. The bond between Christ and the Christian is unbreakable because it is sealed with Christ's blood. Even if our lives are not honoring to him, the Lord will never cast us off. As such, the Christian man and woman must never divorce under any circumstances.

- In the case of a marriage where it is impossible for the Christian couple to live together in harmony, the only option provided in Scripture is separation. This comes with strict conditions on the parties:

- "To the married I give this command (not I but the Lord): A wife must not separate from her husband; but if she does, she must remain unmarried or be reconciled to her husband; and a husband must not divorce his wife." (1 Cor. 7:10)

So as you can see the Lord does not like divorce and there are severe consequences to it that hurt people and children for the rest of their lives. Today most Christians agree that in the case of infidelity or abuse that divorce is permissible. While that is mainly accepted I know personally of men and women that stayed married to their spouse through infidelity and even abuse and were able to bring their spouse back to the Lord through repentance of what they did and now have good and even great marriages. It did take a lot of work, but pressing through is worth it to be able to see what an amazing testimony of loving someone like Christ loved the church can do.

One man was told by the Lord that he would love his wife like Christ loved the church before they were married. Then after they were married she was verbally, physically

59

and sexually abusive to him for what turned out to be almost seven years of marriage. The Lord finally told him to separate so He could finish the work in her that He had started and the Lord would bless him greatly in ministry. Unfortunately she would not change and ultimately divorced him because she could not stand the fact that she could not control him anymore after he separated. But after they were divorced she began to see how much the Lord was blessing him in ministry and she knew she made a major mistake. When the Lord has a strong calling to keep a couple together He will usually make circumstances such in the life of a person to get them to come back to Him to complete His original plan as long as the other party continues to stand in faith and is directed by the Lord.

Sometimes enduring great strife and pain comes at a cost to our esteem and entire being, but when we look at our spouse like Jesus sees them – then we see them through His eyes instead of our own. Then we can have compassion and see that they were hurt by their father and/or mother and other spouses that rejected them through divorce because they were not willing to endure intense pain and suffering to the end. The Lord will bless you amazingly if you do not give up and end the relationship. Extreme sacrifice and tribulation that is willingly endured by someone for another usually equates to an extreme anointing in ministry to change thousands of lives. It can be extremely hard when that person does not change day after day, month after month and year after year and even gets more controlling, demanding and abusive. There will be times that you say out loud, "God – I can't do this anymore!" and when you do – think about what Jesus did for us as he took lash after lash over and over when He had the ability to just speak a word and be taken from the abuse He gave Himself up for. If Jesus can do it....so can you. At times it will be the hardest thing in the world that you will do, but remember as you endure it your spirit will gain strength and the Lord will eventually bless you greatly for your sacrificing of your life and laying it down.

John 15:12-15 NJKV, "[12] This is My commandment, that you love one another as I have loved you. [13] Greater love has no one than this, than to lay down one's life for his friends. [14] You are My friends if you do whatever I command you. [15] No longer do I call you servants, for a servant does not know what his master is doing; but I have called you friends, for all things that I heard from My Father I have made known to you."

When we give up our life's comforts, peace and desires for a season we will become a closer friend of the Lord and there is nothing that He will not do to bless and honor you for your sacrifice. The greater the suffering for another person the greater the favor that He will bless you with both here on earth as well as when you get to heaven as long as you do not complain constantly throughout the season. To truly become like Christ requires that we go through suffering and persecution, and although it is not fun to have your main persecutor be your spouse – many times that is exactly the case.

One thing to also remember is that if you have ever had sexual relations with a person that was not your wife or husband during your life, you would have made a covenant with them through that sexual union which would need to be severed; because any of the sin in those relationships bring curses on your life and would follow you. So speak out loud "I sever all covenants that I have ever made with any other people in my life and cancel all curses that have come into my life because of my sin." It is important to realize this because many are aware of a soul tie needing to be broken; but a soul tie can be with anyone that you do not have sexual intimacy with such as your boss or manager at work or a co-worker that was a very close friend.

Many actions we take in life produce ramifications of which we are never aware. We don't realize them because no one ever taught us of the consequences and how they affect us throughout our lives. The Lord knew what He was doing when He created us and that His only intentions were to have one woman marry one man for life. Satan is in this world to hurt men and women and to try to get us off track and to look at each other as the enemy and cause divorce, strife and all kinds of other evil and to take us to hell with him. So keep in mind that all arguing comes because of the enemy in either the husband or wife's life and often times both at the same time. Know who the real enemy is and always have your mate's back both in prayer and in support. In the movie *Fireproof* the main character played by Kirk Cameron states, "Never leave your partner behind." If only both people in marriage would have this mantra burned into their memories so that they would remember it above all that the enemy may say to them. If you never left your partner behind you would never even consider a divorce. The enemy is behind every divorce – do not even let the word divorce be spoken from your mouth much less dwell on it in your mind for even a second. The enemy is the enemy. Fight for your mate and help them to be healed from the enemy.

Chapter 5

Step by Step

Since so many families have been broken by the enemy there is an imperative need to discuss how to love stepchildren like Christ. It is always easier to forgive your own child for doing something that was not right or costs you money then it is someone else's child. So how do we get to the point where we can overlook an offense by our stepchildren instead of verbally berating them for behavior that is not godly or not beneficial to us or our family?

Seeing them through the eyes of Christ is much easier said than done. What would you do if you were asleep in bed at 11:30 p.m. the night before Easter and your stepson called your wife and asked her to come pick him up from a city almost three hours away because his car would not start after attending a sporting event? You knew that his mother had a friend that lived in the city where her son was stranded, so asked if she could call her and see if her son and his girlfriend could stay there so that you could go pick them up the next day. Your wife then called her friend at almost midnight and they had no problem driving thirty minutes to go pick up your stepson and his girlfriend so that everyone could have a decent sleep. Unfortunately your stepson did not want to stay at his mother's friend's home because he said his girlfriend's father was an ex-Marine. The ex-Marine did not like him and would yell at him if he did not get her home that very night because he was not supposed to have taken her that far away from home to begin with.

So his mother (your wife) was all ready to get out of bed and call a tow truck service to have him towed to a city two and a half hours away from where you lived and drive to that city to pick him up so he would not have to be yelled at by his girlfriend's father. So what do you do? Do you let your wife drive by herself in the wee hours of the morning to go "rescue" her oldest son so that he will not have to face consequences? Or do you get up and lose an entire night's sleep to help? The boy's stepfather reluctantly got out of bed and drove his wife two and a half hours to pick up his stepson and his girlfriend arriving around 3:00 a.m. Everything in him wanted to lash out verbally to scold him for not staying with his wife's friend so he could have slept and picked him up the next day. Instead, the Lord told him to say no harsh words to him as his stepson looked impishly guilty when he arrived as he got in his stepfather's vehicle with his girlfriend. The stepfather then drove them all the way back home arriving around 6:00 a.m. as the sun began to rise and his wife, stepson and girlfriend were fast asleep in the car. He said nothing harsh to the stepson and went to sleep once he arrived home and ended up missing Easter services. He never spoke one word of criticism to his stepson as he gave him what he felt like was some extreme grace.

That is one example of loving a person like Christ loved the church as the stepfather gave his life up for the actions of his stepson. Everything in this man's flesh wanted to yell at his stepson and tell him how selfish he was for not staying with his mother's friend and making him exhausted for not sleeping at all and then missing the entire Easter service at church all because his stepson did not want to be yelled at by his girlfriend's father for taking her that far away and not getting her back when he should have. Instead he did not get into strife – bit his tongue – and said to himself – the reason why this young man behaved this way is because he was hurt by his father divorcing his mother when he was just five years old, and he is behaving this way out of the pain that he suffered years ago. So he gave it to the Lord and let it go and never said a word of correction to his stepson because he could not have handled hearing it and would have taken an offense against his stepfather.

Another man was told by the Lord to lend his expensive SUV to his stepson so he could work at a job that required it. The man worked from his home so he could still do his job without his vehicle, but he was inconvenienced if he ever needed to get a haircut as he would have to walk two miles to town instead of drive as well as other delays and logistic challenges. The Lord did not tell him how long it would be, but the man was expecting that his stepson would be able to buy his own car within a couple of months after he made more money from his new job. He only asked the son to change the oil whenever it needed it and make sure the air pressure in the tires was where it should be. What started out to be just a few weeks turned into a few months. The stepson did not make enough money from his sales to buy his own vehicle. Eventually the vehicle was driven over some nails and one of them got lodged in the tire and kept losing air from the hole. The man asked his stepson nicely to please take care of it, but the stepson did not – so eventually his mother took it in after several days and got it patched. Also, the two months of giving up his most prized possession of his vehicle turned into six months and eventually needed the oil changed, but the stepson did not change the oil. After being asked several times the stepson still did not change it, so his mother took it in to get the oil changed. This frustrated the stepfather because he wanted his wife's son to learn responsibility yet could not get him to do the right thing.

One time at Christmas the man's stepson decided to watch a couple of dogs for his friend and put them into his stepfather's SUV without asking him to drive to his home. The stepfather was not pleased when he saw dogs running outside of his home in the backyard as he knew he had to have transported them in his SUV. Sure enough the SUV smelled like dogs and had a lot of mud that the dogs tracked into the vehicle that the stepson would not clean out. Also the stepson would eat sunflower seeds and had spilled many of them in the vehicle over the months he drove it. Finally, after nine months of driving the SUV, the stepfather told his stepson that he needed to purchase his own car with his tax refund. The stepson agreed that he would get his own car, although he needed another $2,000 with which to get a vehicle, so the stepfather agreed to loan him the additional money he needed. The stepson was not responsible in keeping the vehicle in good repair or obeying the requests of the stepfather, but the Lord told the stepfather that because of all the rejection the stepson received from his father and living in dysfunction that he was incapable of being in a position to behave like he was supposed to due to the trauma he experienced growing up. Therefore the man needed to give his stepson extra grace. Grace means unmerited favor. It is not deserved yet is given.

Another man allowed his stepson to live in his wife's former home, but instead of paying rent at market price (around $1,200 a month) he only charged him $400 initially for 4 years because the stepson did not want his older brother living with him as he did not get along with him. The only utilities the stepfather had him pay were for cable TV – as the stepson could not afford to pay for the electric or water bill. Eventually the stepson purchased a 3D TV that he could not afford on a monthly payment plan and after a year could not afford to pay for it anymore, so a collections agency was going to hurt his credit if he did not pay for what he owed. So the stepfather stepped in and paid it off for him - $1,700 - even though he could not afford to pay for it either. He prayed about it and the Lord instructed him to give his stepson extra grace due to the pain that he suffered from his father divorcing his mother years before.

One stepmother decided to use some extra bonus money from her husband to purchase a newer car for her stepson. She found the car on Craigslist and over the 4th of July she and her husband test drove it and bought it. Then they surprised her stepson with it and he was so grateful and shocked. So they exchanged the car that he had been driving (an older model Nissan Sentra) to take it upon themselves to share to drive until her husband made enough from another bonus a month later to purchase a newer car for herself.

One man paid for over $85,000 worth of various expenses for his two stepsons including school loan bills, reduced monthly rent, utilities, vehicles, food, entertainment and other expenses over a five year span while paying minimal expenses for his own three children and chose not to tell his own children why he could no longer afford to take them out to eat or to buy them clothes because he knew that would cause his children to resent his stepsons as well as his new wife. So he just told them that things were a little tight and that he could not afford to buy them things like he used to and took the blame instead of telling the truth of the situation. He shielded his stepsons and wife from the jealousy, anger and hatred that would have ensued had he shared the truth with his own children why he could no longer afford to purchase them things. He also avoided his own children being angry with their stepmother for being the cause of the lack of money. More grace that was extended that the Lord had instructed which was not easy to do whatsoever because the stepfather ended up going into $50,000 worth of debt on credit cards because of this extreme sacrificial act of love like Christ. Two years later the Lord rewarded the man by having him lose his job due to downsizing and then received a net severance check for exactly $50,000 so he could pay off all of his credit card debt. Then the

67

Lord brought him a new job that paid him more than his previous job.

One stepmother learned that her stepdaughter decided to have a New Year's eve party when she and her husband were out of town attending a Christian conference in Orlando, FL. Those that attended the house party wrote and drew pictures on the stepdaughter's wall - various things that were not godly - and someone had even broken into their master bedroom. Upon their return home the stepmother and her husband had a very calm discussion with her stepdaughter and she showed tremendous remorse for what she did and agreed to paint her room to cover up the writings and drawings that were inappropriate. Instead of losing her cool at her stepdaughter she gave her grace and loved on her knowing that the enemy was behind what happened as she was not a bad person. This kept the relationship between the two stronger instead of potentially damaging it forever had she said what the enemy wanted her to speak to her stepdaughter. Grace.

These are all acts of love that a godly parent took upon themselves and suffered while showing the love of Christ to their stepchildren. Unfortunately so many stepparents get angry when it costs them money to have to pay for the irresponsibility of another child that is not their own, but what does Jesus call us to do? To lay our lives down. What does laying one's life down mean? To put someone else's needs, wants and desires in front of our own and not be able to satisfy our own while not complaining about it to them afterwards is what Christ is talking about. It is so easy to love someone that does what we want them to do, but the true calling of a Christ-like person is to not say a word to a stepchild who is behaving in a way that is not the way they should perform and allow their own parent to correct them or at least be very careful to only correct them in a most gentle and loving way. Grace is not easy and requires much discipline over our mouths but over time will work to help change a person from irresponsible behavior to responsible as they see it modeled in front of them.

If a child cannot take any correction whatsoever without being hurt and immediately takes offense, then it may take much more sacrifice on your part, biting your tongue constantly and not listening to the enemy whisper in your ear to speak out what your flesh may be screaming to say to them or that you may even say to your own children. You may need to go the extra, extra mile to love on them and sometimes let them make decisions that cause you stress, inconvenience and even cost you thousands and thousands of dollars in order to help them heal from their past trauma.

Loving your stepchildren means being tuned in to God when the enemy speaks to you about what he wants you to speak out to correct them. Instead of following the voice of the enemy, say "No" and remain calm and see them through the eyes of Christ; have compassion for them and extend to them much grace. Once you have built a relationship with them (and it could take five or more years to do so depending on how much they were hurt by their father or mother and how old they are when you married their mother or father), then you can slowly provide them with instruction and guidance in a loving tone. If you have a challenge with speaking harsh words out to them, then pray that you change and are able to see them like Jesus does. The Holy Spirit will reveal to you the pains that are in their hearts from their past and give you the patience to love them like Jesus.

One stepson whose mother divorced his stepfather continued to maintain a healthy relationship with his stepfather because he knew from all the love that he was shown over the previous seven years that his stepfather was the real deal and exemplified the love from the Father; and that no matter how much his mother spoke false negative words about his stepfather to him, he knew the truth and loved him because he could feel the genuine godly love from him. The enemy tries to sever relationships and speak lies, but the Holy Spirit that lives in someone can sense the truth and produce healthy relationships for a lifetime regardless of the words spoken from a parent that are untrue to their child. Truth can try to be masked by

69

the enemy in someone; but eventually it comes out even though it may take many months or even years for the Lord to reveal it. The truth always comes out eventually as the Holy Spirit reveals it.

Chapter 6

So What Does the Bible Say?

What are we instructed to do in the Bible when it comes to dealing with people who are challenging to love? Unconditional love is caring about someone without strings attached; loving without conditions and doing something to cause someone to be blessed or receive grace without any thought for what we might receive back ourselves or what will be involved in our sacrifice. For most people this is very rare behavior because giving of ourselves to the point where we are hurting is not easy nor what our flesh wants to do, but it is what Jesus exemplified. It is uncommon to receive kindness without it costing us something in return. This type of love involves risk and a willingness to fail as we give ourselves over with total vulnerability. It is putting our own needs and pride behind us and doing what is best for someone else regardless of how we feel, knowing that we may be taken advantage of. It requires staying close to someone; not judging, punishing or condemning them but loving without conditions. This type of love has the power to heal deep wounds, change lives and destinies and create powerful relationships beyond our capacity to imagine. So what are some ways that the Bible says to love?

1) **Forgive:** Forgiveness is a choice, and not a feeling, which takes time and prayer. Jesus said we are to forgive someone 70 x 7 in Matthew 18:22 (NKJV)
"Jesus said to him, "I do not say to you, up to seven times, but up to seventy times seven." To fully understand what Jesus was saying, we must look at the context of the whole chapter, for Jesus was speaking not only about forgiving one another but about Christian character, both in and out of the church. The admonition to forgive our brother seventy times seven follows Jesus' discourse on discipline in the church (Matthew 18:15-20), in which He lays down the rules for restoring a sinning brother.

By saying we are to forgive those who sin against us seventy times seven, Jesus was not limiting forgiveness to 490 times, a number that is, for all practical purposes, beyond counting. Christians with forgiving hearts not only do not limit the number of times they forgive; they continue to forgive with as much grace the thousandth time as they do the first time. Christians are only capable of this type of forgiving spirit because the Spirit of God lives within us, and it is He who provides the ability to offer forgiveness over and over, just as God forgives us over and over. We are never to take an offense against someone and if they do something that hurts us deeply we are to let it go and forgive. Never ruminate upon it for days, weeks, months, years or a lifetime because it will hurt you and can cause all kinds of sickness and diseases as it open up a door to the enemy to have a right to hurt you.

Be unable to be offended, recognizing that they are doing things out of their pain and that is not who they really would be had they not been hurt. Ephesians 4:30-32 NKJV,

"[30] And do not grieve the Holy Spirit of God, by whom you were sealed for the day of redemption. [31] Let all bitterness, wrath, anger, clamor, and evil speaking be put away from you, with all malice. [32] And be kind to one another, tenderhearted, forgiving one another, even as God in Christ forgave you."

2) **Sacrifice:** Putting our own needs, desires and wants aside to focus on other people's needs and wants. This can be as simple as allowing someone to choose where they want to eat instead of arguing with them to get our way. Or getting up at 6:00 am on a Saturday morning in order to drive to a softball game an hour away just so your stepson can see their daughter as you babysit for them while they play a game in a cold rain. It means not being able to pay for your own bills because you had to help pay for your stepdaughter's bills or else she would receive threatening calls from a bill collector. Sacrifice requires a positive attitude and an obedient heart. Romans 12:1 NKJV, "I beseech you therefore, brethren, by the mercies of God, that you present your bodies as a living sacrifice, holy, acceptable to God, which is your reasonable service."

3) **Pray:** Praying for people is an act of unconditional love. Especially when we pray for those who are hard to love and offend us and cause pain and sacrifice in our lives. This allows us to lift others up to God in a positive manner, asking God to bless people and work in their hearts and lives according to His plan and purposes. Matthew 5:43-48 NKJV, "[43] You have heard that it was said, 'You shall love your neighbor and hate your enemy.' [44] But I say to you, love your enemies, bless those who curse you, do good to those who hate you, and pray for those who spitefully use you and persecute you, [45] "that you may be sons of your Father in heaven; for He makes His sun rise on the evil and on the good, and sends rain on the just and on the unjust. [46] For if you love those who love you, what reward have you? Do not even the tax collectors do the same? [47] And if you greet your brethren only, what do you do more than others? Do not even

the tax collectors do so? [48] "Therefore you shall be perfect, just as your Father in heaven is perfect."

4) **Be Humble:** Living with a humble opinion of ourselves takes us off our own minds and from holding a first place position and puts others in front. Humility teaches us that God created us for His purposes and not our own. It means putting others before us and not bragging on our own accomplishments but letting others discover them on their own. This can be very hard for us as we want people to know about what we are doing; especially with how prevalent social media is today. We need to become peacemakers, recognizing every person has a purpose and needs to be treated with dignity and respect no matter what position they have in society. Being humble requires saying "No" to sinful behavior or responses that want to challenge our "Christ-like" attitude. Arrogance and pride is the opposite of being humble and is the norm amongst people in today's world. We need to remove all pride from our lives because it keeps us from the intimacy with the Lord.

Ephesians 5:25-29 NKJV states "[25] Husbands, love your wives, just as Christ also loved the church and gave Himself for her, [26] that He might sanctify and cleanse her with the washing of water by the word, [27] that He might present to Himself a glorious church, not having spot or wrinkle or any such thing, but that she should be holy and without blemish. [28] So husbands ought to love their own wives as their own bodies; he who loves his wife loves himself. [29] For no one ever hated His own flesh, but nourishes and cherishes it, just as the Lord does the church."

A man is called to love his wife by giving himself up for her. What does that mean? It means that he will give up many of his own desires for his wife. He will go the extra mile and show her as Christ did, what it is like to help her feel treasured and loved unconditionally. When she prefers to eat at a certain restaurant he wants to eat at another he defers to her without striving. When she is cold and needs another blanket at night he gets up and retrieves it for her. When she needs comforted he puts his arms around her and tells her he loves her. When she is cold at night he puts his arm around her in bed and holds her tightly. It is a sacrificial love that he puts his own personal desires on hold to love her perfectly like Christ would. When she is in fear he battles for her in the spirit to help her keep her peace. When she is worried about finances he does not get into fear but listens to the Lord and He directs and then he leads her accordingly. He reads the Word and does what it says. He prays in the spirit and says no harsh words to her no matter what she does to him. He will suffer long for her helping her through all of her past wounds in life and does not give up and will not divorce her unless all other options fail. He loves her like Christ would.

John 13:34-35 NKJV states, "[34] A new commandment I give to you, that you love one another; as I have loved you, that you also love one another. [35] By this all will know that you are My disciples, if you have love for one another."

As most of us are raised by parents that did not love us totally unconditionally or teach us what Christ truly meant – it becomes a journey to learn just what that means that Jesus referred to. Most of us have limited tolerances for one another that are not the same as what Jesus stated, and many have no idea what it is like to love like Jesus. They easily become offended over another person's behaviors that infringe on their ability to live their life like they want and then they speak out words of correction in harshness that hurt the person even more causing them to be driven away from the Lord as they do not want what you have. And many that are in the church today think that they know how to love like Christ yet are very condemning and condescending in their views of hurting people instead of loving them unconditionally. Our old selfish mindsets have to die and new Christ-like love must emerge.

Ephesians 5:1-2 NKJV says, "[1] Therefore be imitators of God as dear children. [2] And walk in love, as Christ has loved us and given

Himself for us, an offering and a sacrifice to God for a sweet-smelling aroma."

How can we imitate God if our earthly father modeled an image of harshness, distance, rejection, control and nothing like the love of God? That is why so many billions of people on earth do not imitate the love of our heavenly Father as they never experienced the unconditional love of God. How can anyone walk in love as an offering or sacrifice to God that smells sweet if they have never experienced it from their own earthly father? That is the challenge that we have as we can only do this if we have a life changing experience and have an emotional heart transplant from our growing up years to our current life. So how does one do that? By asking Father God to let us experience who He really is and to let us hear His voice and to have His son Jesus Christ envelop our spirits with His love. The only way we can possibly love like God desires us to and how Christ led is to exchange all our pains for all His gain that He freely gives to us.

The Holy Spirit is someone you must have in your life, and if you have never asked to receive your prayer language (tongues) I would highly, highly, highly recommend asking the Lord for that gift. It will transform you from your past to who you are in Christ in a way that you could never do on your own or with some self-help class or seminar. I personally pray in my prayer language an hour or more a day as it brings in such a warm peace and gives me a boldness in Christ at the same time. The enemy cannot interfere with you by giving you thoughts of offense, anger, fear or anything while speaking in tongues but love, joy and peace as you become more like Christ. I have seen people who I have counseled around the country that were in constant fear and anger transform quickly into a peaceful person who has patience and love for others like they have never seen. Praying in your prayer language also causes the enemy's voice to disappear from you because you cannot be thinking of anything he has been speaking to you as you are praying in tongues. It gives you an amazing tool in your tool belt of spiritual power against the plans of the enemy.

Philippians 2:1-11 NKJV, "[1] Therefore if there is any consolation in Christ, if any comfort of love, if any fellowship of the Spirit, if any affection and mercy, [2] fulfill my joy by being like-minded, having the same love, being of one accord, of one mind. [3]

76

Let nothing be done through selfish ambition or conceit, but in lowliness of mind let each esteem others better than himself. [4] Let each of you look out not only for his own interests, but also for the interests of others. [5] Let this mind be in you which was also in Christ Jesus, [6] who, being in the form of God, did not consider it robbery to be equal with God, [7] but made Himself of no reputation, taking the form of a bondservant, and coming in the likeness of men. [8] And being found in appearance as a man, He humbled Himself and became obedient to the point of death, even the death of the cross. [9] Therefore God also has highly exalted Him and given Him the name which is above every name, [10] that at the name of Jesus every knee should bow, of those in heaven, and of those on earth, and of those under the earth, [11] and that every tongue should confess that Jesus Christ is Lord, to the glory of God the Father."

So to love like Christ we essentially must transform our old, selfish, flesh-serving lives and minds into that of Christ's. We should not have any selfish bone in our bodies – thus the things that we want we must be willing to sacrifice in order to help others that are hurting to become healed. We must not have any pride in ourselves and if we do we must command that spirit to go from us. The spirit of Leviathan is a very prideful spirit (Job 41) and can be very hard to get set free from if we have operated in it for a lifetime. It is usually developed through not receiving unconditional love from our father or could be from a curse that came down our family lines from anyone involved in Freemasons, Scottish Rite or the Shriners. I talk extensively about that spirit and have powerful deliverance prayers that have seen immediate results in my book *Restored to Freedom*.

We are not to pay attention and solely focus on our own interests but are to look at those who are hurting (bleeding in their hearts) to love on them. Can you become as a bondservant? What exactly is a bondservant? The definition is a person bound in service without wages. It means to deliberately sign away my own rights to receive payment in order to complete the requirements of the job. The term bondservant in the New Testament is a translation of the Greek word *doulos*. Unlike perceptions of modern slavery, bondservant or *doulos* is a relatively broad term with a wider range of usage. In the time of the New Testament a bondservant could refer at times to someone who voluntarily served others. In most cases the term referred to a person in a permanent role of servitude. A bondservant was considered the property of a Roman citizen, holding no right to leave his place of service. Some historians believe that one-third of the Roman population lived as bondservants. Jews owned bondservants or slaves. In contrast with the cultural view, Jesus taught that the greatest was the "servant (*doulos*) of all" in Mark 9:35. So for us to live as a bondservant to Christ means that we are to treat all in our lives like Christ did. Not to have certain types of people that we prefer to love on and then ignore others. Too many Christians look down upon the less fortunate instead of loving them like Christ would and just pass it off as "I just do not want to be around everyone." They would walk past someone in the road that needed care unlike what the good Samaritan did in the Bible. Be like the Samaritan and love on ALL that need help and love.

Philippians 4:8-9 NKJV, "[8] Finally, brethren, whatever things are true, whatever things are noble, whatever things are just, whatever things are pure, whatever things are of good report, if there is anything praiseworthy – meditate on these things. [9] The things which you learned and received and heard and saw in me, these do, and the God of peace will be with you."

When you are around people that have been hurt they will be speaking words of death and not life. By the mere fact that you will be spending time (and perhaps living with) these people you will be tempted to come down to their level and look at all the negatives in your life. You cannot do this because life and death is in the power of your tongue. So focus on things that are noble, just, pure, of good report and praise Him because that will keep you from being lured into the enemy's traps and losing your peace and getting into anger or fear. Rejoice in the Lord always and again I say rejoice. Then when you are around the people that are hurting - you will affect them positively and they will eventually change over time (and it could take years to undo all the damage from the enemy over a lifetime).

Galatians 5:22-26 NKJV, "[22] But the fruit of the Spirit is love, joy, peace, longsuffering, kindness, goodness, faithfulness, [23] gentleness, self-control. Against such there is no law. [24] And those who are Christ's have crucified the flesh with its passions and desires. [25] If we live in the Spirit, let us also walk in the Spirit. [26] Let

78

us not become conceited, provoking one another, envying one another."

So if we have the Holy Spirit inside of us helping us to behave like Christ, then we should display the fruit with behavior consistent with the above scripture. If we have anything else coming out of us then we typically would be affected by an enemy spirit (and perhaps several) from our past that needs to be removed through commanding it out as well as changing our old mindsets to that of Christ. Walking in love, joy and peace is such a freeing and amazing feeling that far too many Christians do not know and far more non-Christians never experience.

Many do not want to experience that most amazing fruit of the spirit called longsuffering. Anything with the word suffer does not usually conjure up thoughts of relaxing on the beach in Bora Bora. What does it mean to long suffer or suffer long? This word is made up of two Greek words meaning "long" and "temper"; literally meaning "long-tempered." So then to be longsuffering is to have self-restraint when one is being provoked to anger. Has anyone that is hard to love ever tried to provoke you to anger? In my life I saw it thousands of times over about a 17 year period with my son, wife and stepsons. With my own son I was not very good at keeping my calm and often times was provoked to a verbal escalation in my fervor with him. With my second wife and her sons I became much more Christ-like only by the total grace of God as I could feel my whole personality and spirit change prior to my getting married. I was able to bite my tongue with much more consistent regularity when everything in my flesh was screaming to speak out. Was I able to not respond in frustration every time I was provoked? Absolutely not – but I was able to limit losing control with a much higher frequency through looking at their behavior with Christ's eyes and having compassion on them instead of allowing myself to hate them for what they were doing to cause me pain and cause me to have to sacrifice most all that I desired.

A longsuffering person does not immediately retaliate or punish; rather the person has a "long fuse" and is very patient. They can take horrible verbal assaults every day, week, month and year and try to eventually move away from the barrage to another room when able or walk away from the person so that they can remain in peace; because once you get pulled into the verbal war then an argument will break out and there is nothing you can do to get your peace back for sometimes hours later or even days.

God is the source of longsuffering because it is part of His character (Exodus 34:6; Numbers 14:18-20; Psalm 86:15; Romans 2:4; 1 Peter 3:9; 2 Peter 3:15). He is very patient with sinners as He could kill us at any moment yet waits until we come to Him at the right time, which could be 50+ years later. While eventually God's longsuffering could come to an end, as seen in the destruction of Sodom and Gomorrah (Genesis 18-19) and in the New Testament in Revelation 2 when discussing how he gave those operating in the spirit of Jezebel time to repent but finally had to put them on a sickbed and kill their children (which are those that they taught to become like them) because they were teaching people things that were drawing them away from God.

So think about how different this world would be if everyone exhibited long suffering through being patient like Christ with others' behaviors that cause so many to become offended. The spirit of offense is everywhere - seemingly growing in strength since the 1990's as so many people shifted away from the Lord and focused inwardly on their own selfish desires as the music industry seemed to change dramatically focusing on self-serving love instead of on others. Individual relationships, family relationships, church relationships and those in the workplace have been wrecked with so many people being offended. In our past ungodly, old nature we would tend to be very short with people and strike back against offenses with negative and provoking words and unforgiving spirits. By listening to the Holy Spirit and becoming like Christ we can say "No" to the enemy's voice in our heads and forgive the other person and behave extremely patiently with them, never taking an offense.

We should never strive with anyone ever; which means not provoking someone to become angry when we know how sensitively they would normally behave. That takes discernment on our part to recognize what a person can handle and what they cannot. If you are dealing with a mature Christian you should be able to lovingly speak a word of correction to them, if they should need correcting, without them losing control and getting angry and raging against you. If you are working with a less mature Christian you may have to sugar-coat and soften your message to them and perhaps avoid it altogether if you know it will set them off like a bomb. There are some who have been in the church for 40+ years that are still not mature in their Christian walk and you have to stay away from subjects that will cause them to become angry. Yes, it is frustrating to not be able to talk about certain areas with all Christians, but the Holy Spirit will tell you what they are capable of handling and what they cannot. Loving like Christ means knowing who can handle what and what the delivery needs to be to get across the message most effectively and safely.

2 Timothy 2:23-26 NKJV, "[23] But avoid foolish and ignorant disputes, knowing that they generate strife. [24] And a servant of the Lord must not quarrel but be gentle to all, able to teach, patient, [25] in humility correcting those who are in opposition, if God perhaps will grant them repentance, so that they may know the truth, [26] and that they may come to their senses and escape the snare of the devil, having been taken captive by him to do his will."

I sometimes like to compare the standard language in the NKJV with the Message Bible as it is usually more plainly stated and to the point and easier to understand.

2 Timothy 2:22-26 Message, "Run away from infantile indulgence. Run after mature righteousness – faith, love, peace – joining those who are in honest and serious prayer before God. Refuse to get involved in inane discussions; they always end up in fights. God's servant must not be argumentative, but a gentle listener and a teacher who keeps cool, working firmly but patiently with those who refuse to obey. You never know how or when God might sober them up with a change of heart and a turning to the truth, enabling them to escape the Devil's trap, where they are caught and held captive, forced to run his errands."

How many of you have ever read these passages before in the Message version? I had not until the writing of this book. It states not to get involved in "inane discussions." Inane means silly, stupid, senseless or absurd. Another definition is empty or void. In other words – it is a total waste of energy and time to get involved in silly or stupid discussions and can leave you feeling empty and void because "they always end up in fights!" I have seen this play out so many times in my own life. Especially when you are in marriage to someone or have a child that is not in the right space as far as living in peace and living a life close to the Lord. The enemy that is speaking to them will try to provoke you into an argument and if you take the bait and try to "set them straight" your initial "discussion" will escalate into an argument and once you have lost your peace it could take many hours if not days to get it back. So if you can just avoid ALL potential major disagreements by saying to the provoking party "Sorry, but I have to go," due to myriad reasons and then "get out of Dodge" with your peace intact. It is not worth it to try to correct a person that you know is not speaking accurately if they are going to lose their cool and go off on you verbally. It is better to let them think they are right and keep the peace. Yes, it is extremely frustrating on those of us that know the truth of a matter or situation, to allow someone who is clearly not correct to think they are, but that is what we are called to do as a true Christian in order to stay out of strife and the enemy's lair. Just say "No" to offense and strife no matter what it may feel like to your flesh.

Luke 17:1-4 NKJV, "[1] Then He said to the disciples, 'It is impossible that no offenses should come, but woe to him through whom they do come! [2] It would be better for him if a millstone were hung around his neck, and he were thrown into the sea, than that he should offend one of these little ones. [3] Take heed to yourselves. If your brother sins against you, rebuke him; and if he repents forgive him. [4]And if he sins against you seven times in a day, and seven times in a day returns to you, saying "I repent," you shall forgive him."

The first part of this scripture states that if you offend a little one that you should have a very heavy stone tied around your neck and then be drowned in the sea. How many parents hurt their children with their words and cause enormous damage to the child as they grow up as they have repeated verbal wounds that hurt them and develop in the child a spirit of anger and hatred. If they attend church, then their children would want nothing to do with "their God" as they see such a hypocritical life being lived out before them. So the Lord is not pleased when a person who is supposed to be mature in their Christian walk causes one who is not mature to be offended.

In the second part of the scripture it refers to someone who is a brother – which perhaps we can interpret as a fellow believer who is somewhat mature in the Lord. If they sin against you (causing an offense) and you confront them for what they did and they genuinely repent and ask for forgiveness, then you should forgive. But let's say that same brother means your husband or wife. What if they say something to hurt you not once in a day but seven times. How many could honestly say that they would forgive them every time all day long for each offense? Most would probably forgive their spouse if they did two and maybe three things to hurt them throughout the day – but seven? Now that is a lot of serious forgiveness that must be given, yet that is what Jesus called us to do. Most would state that he is not just stopping at the number seven but meaning an infinite number of offenses a day. Can you be unable to be offended? No matter what anyone does or says to you – just simply turn the other cheek and go on. It is extremely hard to do when you are not strong in your walk with the Lord – but perhaps the Lord has an extremely anointed ministry waiting for you on the other side of your season of extreme tribulation and if you give up and walk out on this person you will never see it. That is why it is so very important to hear the voice of the Lord, and if you have friends that are reliable at hearing the Lord (prophetic), then ask them what the Lord says to them to confirm what you are hearing. Usually the more intense the suffering and longsuffering that you have to do for someone (or multiple people), the more anointed your ministry will eventually become as long as you do not give up.

Proverbs 19:11 AMP, "Good sense makes a man restrain his anger, and it is his glory to overlook a transgression or an offense."

Having anger is definitely not a fruit of the spirit and taking an offense is a recipe for disaster. Spewing out words of anger can also cause serious physical issues and disease to manifest in the body such as high blood pressure. One must never give in to the enemy and become angry with someone no matter what they may do to you. Once you become angry you give the enemy a right to come in and cause a lot of negative things to happen in your life which will hurt you and others. So ask the Lord to give you more patience and understanding to see the offending person through His eyes and be able to see why they are behaving that way. Then ask Him to change you into receiving more of the spirit of Christ.

The second part of that verse talks about how it is a man's glory to overlook an offense. So at the point that you could choose to become offended and say something negative back in retaliation to the person who hurt you – if you can catch yourself and let it go, then you will bring glory to yourself and to the Lord. The challenge is in actually doing that – how do you not listen and ruminate upon an offense? What if your father-in-law says something that hurts your wife? What should you do? If you bring it up to him, he will probably become offended and may never speak to you again even though your wife is able to simply forgive and forget. Then the next time you get together at your wife's parent's home her father gives you the cold shoulder and is negative towards you. This could go on for years. Or say that your stepson who lives with you cusses at your wife in front of you and you step up and tell him he should not do that ever again and correct him in anger. Now he never wants to talk to you again and treats you in anger for a long season as he hates you as you "offended" him even though what he did was very wrong. You feel like you cannot win for trying and feel like giving up. It is so important to be slow to speak and quick to listen and is such a challenge for step parents when correcting their spouse's children.

One man's son was angry at him because he made him come home one night to his home because it was his week to have his children and his son called him a horrible name. The boy's stepmother got very angry and told him essentially to shut his mouth and respect his father. The next response from the son was that he demanded to be taken to his biological mother's home immediately. He stayed living with her for an entire year before he finally dropped his offense against his new stepmother. So the boy was clearly wrong in what he said yet had his stepmother bit her tongue he would not have lived for a year with his mother and could have seen his dad half of the year. It is such a challenge to know what the right thing is to do in the heat of the battle. What I have learned is that if you can be slow to speak and quick to pray and ask the Lord what to do, normally the response will be to say nothing or to be very loving back and then later at the right time when everyone is calm you can address the matter more wisely.

James 1:19 NKJV, "[19] So then, my beloved brethren, let every man be swift to hear, slow to speak, slow to wrath; [20] for the wrath of man does not produce the righteousness of God."

This verse is so easy to read yet so hard to do when someone that is being affected by a spirit is speaking to you angrily; especially when you have historically been quick to speak and fast to get angry due to seeing your father or mother behaving and modeling this behavior which you have been emulating for most of your lifetime. So how do you do this practically? The first step is getting free from being angry which may involve commanding old familiar spirits to go from you. If you have a spirit of anger and have no patience, then you must be loosed from that spirit. The most effective way is to simply speak out loud "I command you spirit of anger to go from me now in Jesus' name!" You may also want to break off any generational curses (the prayers are in my book *Restored to Freedom*) that could be affecting you if others in your family get angry often. Once you are free from that you will have a much easier time with staying in peace. Then it is a matter of staying in peace and if ever you feel anything that is taking you away from your peace you are to bind and rebuke that spirit from you (fear, depression, anger, etc) or try to walk away from the person that is striving with you until they are calm again. Praying in your prayer language is another great tactic to help you stay in peace and get the enemy out of your head because you cannot hear the enemy's voice (or anything else) when you are praying in tongues.

Have you ever thought about what love really is? The person you are trying to love may have never known what it was because they were never loved, and what they do not possess they cannot give out to anyone else. Do you know what love really is? Let us turn to 1 Corinthians 13:4-13 NKJV

- [4] Love suffers long and is kind; love does not envy; love does not parade itself, is not puffed up;
- [5] does not behave rudely, does not seek its own, is not provoked, thinks no evil;
- [6] does not rejoice in iniquity, but rejoices in the truth;
- [7] bears all things, believes all things, hopes all things, endures all things.
- [8] Love never fails. But whether there are prophecies, they will fail; whether there are tongues, they will cease; whether there is knowledge, it will vanish away.
- [9] For we know in part and we prophesy in part.

- ^{10} But when that which is perfect has come, then that which is in part will be done away.
- ^{11} When I was a child, I spoke as a child, I understood as a child, I thought as a child; but when I became a man, I put away childish things.
- ^{12} For now we see in a mirror, dimly, but then face to face. Now I know in part, but then I shall know just as I also am known.
- ^{13} And now abide faith, hope, love, these three; but the greatest of these is love.

I love what the Message translation explains as to what love is as it becomes more clear ; 1 Corinthians 13:4-13 below:

- $^{4-7}$ Love never gives up.
- Love cares more for others than for self.
- Love doesn't want what it doesn't have.
- Love doesn't strut,
- Doesn't have a swelled head,
- Doesn't force itself on others,
- Isn't always "me first,"
- Doesn't fly off the handle,
- Doesn't keep score of the sins of others,
- Doesn't revel when others grovel,
- Takes pleasure in the flowering of truth,
- Puts up with anything,
- Trusts God always,
- Always looks for the best,
- Never looks back,
- But keeps going to the end.
- $^{8-10}$ Love never dies.
- Inspired speech will be over some day;
- praying in tongues will end;
- understanding will reach its limit.
- We know only a portion of the truth,
- and what we say about God is always incomplete.

- But when the Complete arrives, our incompletes will be canceled.
- [11] When I was an infant at my mother's breast, I gurgled and cooed like any infant. When I grew up, I left those infant ways for good.
- [12] We don't yet see things clearly. We're squinting in a fog, peering through a mist. But it won't be long before the weather clears and the sun shines bright! We'll see it all then, see it all as clearly as God sees us, knowing Him directly just as He knows us!
- [13] But for right now, until that completeness, we have three things to do to lead us toward that consummation: Trust steadily in God, hope unswervingly, love extravagantly. And the best of the three is love.

So love puts up with anything. What does anything mean? I think it means anything – or everything. Can you put up with anything and everything? For Christ? You can if you choose to and then you can be responsible for changing a soul from a life of sadness and hopelessness into a life of hope and joy. You can help save a life from death and lead them to a life for Christ. What an awesome and amazing responsibility we have as true Christians – to be able to have a relationship with a person that has been so badly hurt by the words of a father or mother, sibling, step parent, teacher, worker, manager, you name it – and then love on them the way Christ wants you to and take any and all hurtful words or actions over a season of perhaps months or years and slowly see them change and blossom into a beautiful and peaceful person. You can do it because Christ's spirit lives in you. You can do it. The only question is – do you want to do it? Will you do it? Will you lay your life down for someone else who is bleeding all over the place and needs you to bite your tongue and come along side of them to help them walk out of the dark clouds of the enemy into the sunshine of the Lord?

There are so many scriptures that deal with not taking offense, staying at peace, loving like Christ loved, sacrificing, giving not expecting anything in return, and not getting angry. Can you bite your tongue and not take the bait from the enemy and retaliate? So in the words of the large athletic ware company from Oregon....JUST DO IT !

Chapter 7

What Did Moses Do?

So when the Lord prompted me to write this book I felt very honored because I could have never written such a book during the earlier years of my life because I did not know how to love like Christ and there was no way that I could actually do it because I would often take offenses when someone did things that I knew were wrong or hurt me. When He told me in January of 2009 that I would love my wife like Christ loved the church I did not know quite what to make of it. I knew it was not my voice that said those words to me because I would have never thought that nor would I have ever thought I was capable of doing it. So I asked the Lord "what does that mean and who can do that?" All that He told me was that I would learn what it meant over time and that I would love like Christ loved the church in every way imaginable as I transformed from my former selfish-flesh life into behaving much more like Christ every day. Over time I learned exactly what it meant and what it required and was so much more challenging then I could have ever imagined.

Essentially it meant laying down all of my own life's desires and wants for other people who were hurt in extreme ways by the enemy through other people. Then I understood that the people who hurt my loved ones were hurt by people in their family and on and on as it went back up the family lineage. It had become a vicious cycle of trauma that caused otherwise good people to be hurt in ways that caused them to act out of fear, to have no trust in godly people, to have a misguided view of the Lord and thus treat other people harshly and strive in fear about many things. The Lord allowed me to see in the Spirit through His eyes as to why people act out of their pain in ways that are not peaceful and loving and out of fear and torment from the enemy. I did not ask the Lord for this level of discernment or gifting but rather He gave me the ability to see it from His perspective at the end of 2008 before I entered into a new relationship. It was really incredible to experience because I changed so dramatically to see others like He saw them that it felt like He unplugged a chip in my brain and plugged in a chip from His brain. I instantly changed and had such extreme patience and could suffer long having compassion for people that few others would want to endure.

When we see with Christ's eyes from His perspective – in the Spirit – then we can have extreme compassion for those who are hurting in this world that take out all their pain on other people who try loving them. I often times wondered why the Lord allowed me to go through this extreme level of love and compassion while I was enduring the trauma and wondered how long would it last before I would see a change. All He would tell me was that "It would be worth it in the end." So in other words, I would find out later and just needed to ride out as best I could the sacrificing of my life for the betterment of others. To allow myself to be transformed through the process of becoming more Christ-like, however long it was to last as He never told me an end date. So what I learned while enduring this season of my life was that when others would rise up in strife or selfish desires, which cost me literally tens of thousands of dollars as well as little enjoyment and no peace in my own life, that it was my assignment from the Lord to endure and not complain to Him about it. I was essentially "taking one for the team" so to say – for the Kingdom of God – and that while I did not know the ending of the game plan I had to completely trust in the Lord that He would protect me and provide for me and I had to stay in faith that one day He would reward me for enduring this extreme tribulation and to see it to conclusion and restoration. My ultimate desire was for those I was loving on to change and be healed so that they could stop being tormented by the enemy and be able to live a productive life in peace, love and joy for Him.

If we are not able to see our season of sacrifice from our spouse, stepchild or other relationships' perspectives then we become intolerant, impatient and angry and all that the Lord wanted to do through us becomes wasted in both our lives and those we were called to help gain their freedom. Instead of being a part of the solution we become a part of the problem. Then the reward that the Father had waiting for you, albeit the cost is great during this season of your life, will not come and you will have missed the opportunity to be blessed in ways too innumerable to count as well as to see your loved ones healed, changed and set free.

Think of the Old Testament men or women of God. I have often times thought of the life of Moses and what he had to endure. He grew up living a life of luxury from the day after he floated down the Nile into the arms of the Egyptian family of Pharaoh. He was treated to a life of being a prince - eating the finest foods, wearing the most beautiful clothes and the only significant challenge he had to deal with was living in competition with Pharaoh's own biological son Rameses II. He was adored by his mother and respected by all who knew him as he was building a city for the Pharaoh.

One day he learned who he truly was - a Hebrew - and then he knew that the gods the Egyptians served were not the God that the Hebrews served. One day, while on his trip to the countryside, he could not control his temper and seeing an Egyptian killing a fellow Hebrew, rose up and wanted to protect him and ended up killing the Egyptian. He then buried the Egyptian's body in the desert hoping no one would find out. Eventually everyone learned of this and Moses knew that Pharaoh was likely to kill him. So to save his own life he fled to Midian across the desert. He was 40 years old when he left. It was there that he came upon seven of Jethro's daughters as a band of crude shepherds came to bully the women to give their own sheep water and make the women wait. Moses protected the women from the men and commanded the men to leave. So you can see through these examples that Moses was called to protect people – even risking his own life for others that he did not know. This is an example of what we are to do when we are called by Christ to love like Him.

So impressed by Moses' act of chivalry, Jethro adopted him as his own son and had his daughter, Zipporah, marry Moses. He was put in charge of watching over Jethro's herds of animals and did so for 40 years! So the first half of his life was living in a palace with the Pharaoh of Egypt, while the next 40 years was living in the wilderness watching over sheep to protect them! He was born into a family that had limited money yet grew up in a life of wealth and luxury which would have led to being proud and needing nothing – yet then changed back to a life of limited income, wealth and tremendous humbleness. As I was writing this book the Lord spoke to me that Moses' life situations were somewhat similar to my own life in that I grew up on a farm with limited money and upon graduation received a job and career that saw an abundance of wealth in my life only to learn who I really was in Christ at age 42 and that I was to become a servant of the Lord to help others who had been hurt. I wanted to protect them and to help them gain their freedom from the enemy. Of course I do not plan on leading a million people across the Red Sea – but I do want to help people gain freedom from all enemy shackles and chains so that they can become free to serve the Lord and become who they are in Christ.

After Moses had been in the wilderness with Jethro for 40 years, he was watching a flock of sheep one day near Mount Horeb when he saw a bush that was on fire but yet was not burning up. Coming closer to it, he began to hear a voice speak to him from it, which was God. God had instructed him to return to Egypt and free the Hebrews from slavery. God taught him to transform a rod into a serpent and also to inflict and heal leprosy. He also blessed him with other amazing power that the Lord would use through him. So think about this – Moses was living a meek but mostly simple and easy life on a farm and could have continued doing so rejecting what God had asked him to do. But instead of choosing the easier life – he agreed to do what God asked him to do – causing him future extreme stress, potential loss of life and extreme sacrifice – all to save people that would eventually turn on him and have no gratefulness for all that he did for them. Does this sound like a choice that you would have made? I know that most people would say "Thanks, but no thanks." But for those who could see others like God saw them – and that God wanted to set them free from their torture and pain – it was a no brainer. Time to pack up and head back to Egypt to get your brother Aaron and demand Pharaoh to "Let my people go!"

We all know how it turned out…after telling the Pharaoh to let his people go, God hardened Pharaoh's heart - I always wondered why God would make Moses' job even harder. The only reason I came up with was to teach everyone who was really in control by showing off with the ten plagues. The plagues which were sent hurt only the Egyptians and didn't touch the Hebrews. Eventually Pharaoh gave up all the Hebrew people and they all left with Moses and crossed over the Red Sea. Then, instead of going straight into the Promised Land, they had to wander in the desert for another 40 years because the people were afraid that the inhabitants of the land promised to them were too big for them to defeat. So think about this: Moses was responsible for over a million people who resented him, grumbled about him, blamed him, treated him with disdain, and worse. No one else wanted to talk to God because they were afraid, so they made Moses their spokesperson yet were disobedient to what the Lord told him that that they should do. It was such a thankless job that I am sure everything in him at times wanted to just let God take them all out – but he even stopped God from doing just that as he thought about what the Egyptians would say if they learned that all the people died by being killed by God after escaping – so God relented.

Have you ever been treated with disrespect, mocked, and cursed, blamed for everything that went wrong – by just one or two of your children or stepchildren or your one spouse? How did it feel? Can you imagine if you had over a million people coming against you? But he was Moses you might say – and to that I would counter with – but he was also human. Therefore if we are only called to endure a challenging person that we are unrelated to for a season of a few months or years (not even 40 years like Moses was called to walk out in) in order to put up with someone that does not deserve anything based on their actions and words to us – then how much more should we be able to withstand and sacrifice for others

93

that are either our offspring or to whom we are married? So get in the habit of biting your tongue the next time you want to cause strife with your spouse, child, stepchild, mother-in-law, father-in-law, co-worker or anyone you meet in life. You should never, ever strive with anyone no matter what. So does that mean that sometimes you will be hurt by the decisions of others and it could cost you thousands and thousands of dollars and you could lose everything that you have ever worked for in your life? Absolutely, positively! Just count it all as joy my friend as you love like Christ, and do it gladly unto the Lord because it will all be worth it in the end.

James 1:2-4 NKJV, "[2] My brethren, count it all joy when you fall into various trials, [3] knowing that the testing of your faith produces patience. [4] But let patience have its perfect work, that you may be perfect and complete, lacking nothing."

Do you think it is a trial when you encounter people in your life that are a challenge to love - even more so when you are married to that person and have to love children that are not your own? So what happens when you have to endure someone that has been hurt by the enemy and acts out behavior that is extremely hard to be around? You must be very, very patient with them. According to verse four it states that when you are patient – a perfect work is being done. To whom? To you! That is right. When you are being pushed to the brink and having to sacrifice greatly – you are being changed into becoming someone that will be perfect and complete – lacking nothing – when that season is over with. You are becoming like Christ! So many people would never put up with living with someone that speaks out horrible words to them over and over and over for sometimes years and years – especially if they never see them change as they give up hope it will ever happen. But if God calls you to do so – then there is a reason for it – and it usually is to help the hurting person eventually get healed but also to see you change into become more like Christ. Yes, you also are being benefitted from the challenge by changing to become more like Christ, and you may not even realize it on your journey due to having to endure what you think is unbearable circumstances. But you must not complain and give up or you will not be able to see your promised land. If you complain, murmur, argue, fight and disobey God – you will lose the gifts that the Lord was going to bless you with. Obviously, if the person you have been called to

94

love on is violent to the point that your life is in danger – you need to seek refuge elsewhere – but short of that you will be amazed at just what you can tolerate and how it will make you a much stronger person for willingly enduring the season of sacrifice.

So Moses' life was essentially broken up into three seasons. Season one was a life of wealth and luxury as he lived as a prince in Egypt. Season two was a season of humbleness when he lived watching over flocks of sheep. Then season three was a season of sacrifice for others – millions of others – who complained and scorned him over and over for 40 years. What was his reward? Unfortunately because he struck the rock instead of speaking to it like God instructed – he was not permitted to walk into his promised land and had to see it from a few miles away (I was fortunate enough to make a visit to that location in 2009 and could see Jericho to the north and the Dead Sea to the south just beyond the desert). Yes, he was rewarded greatly in heaven and will be when the New Jerusalem and kingdom is set up. The Lord wants to bless his children greatly when we agree to sacrifice our lives for others – both here on earth and in heaven and beyond.

So just how do we love like Christ? It is done through a process of transforming our fleshly, selfish desires into godly desires to see others like Christ and God. Seeing past their horrible, selfish behaviors and understanding why they are acting that way – because of the pain inflicted on them from others in their childhood and teenage years. When we see them as they really are called to be and who they will be – and then speak it over their lives to them every day, week and month – and love them like Christ loved the church, laying our lives down for them – then miracles can happen as the hurting people transform from an ugly caterpillar into a beautiful butterfly or an ugly duckling into a majestic swan. While the process may take several years to unfold, it will be worth it in the end. As long as you do not give up.

Chapter 8

What Did Hosea Do?

I strongly recommend reading the whole book of Hosea to anyone who has had to suffer from loving someone who has been a challenge to love as it is just 14 chapters in its entirety and is one of the most amazing stories of sacrifice in the Bible. The name Hosea means "Salvation" or "Deliverance" which is quite appropriate due to what his task was as requested by God. Hosea was chosen by God to live out His message to His people by marrying a woman who would be unfaithful to him. His sensitivity toward the sinful condition of his countrymen and towards the loving heart of God allowed him to take on this very difficult ministry.

Hosea was from the northern kingdom of Israel and ministered to this kingdom soon after the ministry of Amos. Though Israel appeared to have an outward appearance of success, underneath everything spoke of a disaster that was approaching. The people of this period enjoyed peace and prosperity but anarchy was stirring, and it would bring the political collapse of the nation in a few years. The social setting of the nation was filled with corrupt leaders, unstable family life, immorality, and class hatred. Though people continued a form of worship, idolatry was becoming more accepted and the priests were failing to guide the people into ways of righteousness. So in spite of the darkness of the times, Hosea holds out hope that his people will turn back to God.

Essentially, the book of Hosea is about a people who needed to hear about the love of God (sound familiar with the person(s) that you are trying to love yet they are treating you harshly in return?). God wanted to tell them and decided to show them through a demonstration of His love to His people through Hosea. The people thought that love could be bought ("Ephraim had hired lovers" 8:9), that love was the pursuit of self-gratification ("I will go after my lovers who give me," 2:5), and that loving unworthy objects could bring positive benefits ("They became an abomination like the thing they loved," 9:10). God wanted Israel to know how much He loved them in spite of the peoples' running, resisting and rejecting Him. So the problem was how to convey this message of God's love to a people that could not and would not listen. So God's solution was to let a prophet become his own sermon. What an amazing act of giving up one's life for an entire people that the Lord loved. God told Hosea to marry a harlot, love her fully and even have children by her (of which not all turned out to be his), and then go after her and bring her back when she left him for another man. So Hosea was to show by his own love for his wife, Gomer, the kind of love God had for Israel.

How could God possibly want you to suffer unjustly for another person? God told his obedient and faithful prophet Hosea to go out and find a wife. He then added the interesting instruction to Hosea that his wife was to be a prostitute (I am not saying that your spouse is a prostitute, so please do not confuse that with the intent of the story and its relation to someone that is married to a spouse that causes you great suffering, but the sacrifice of loving someone who hurts you deeply is very relevant). Hosea found a prostitute named Gomer with whom he fell in love. He then married her and they had children, although not all of them were his as she had relations with other men during their marriage. Have you ever tried loving children that were not born from you – like stepchildren? It can be the hardest thing you will ever do because you really cannot discipline them the way that you would your own children and they usually push the limits on what they can get away with due to knowing that you cannot discipline them.

Unfortunately Gomer found her life being a stay at home housewife and mother boring and she longed for the old days of excitement and living life by the seat of her pants with other men. There were no thrills with her present life so she returned to the old one and began having relations with other men; which you can imagine how much that would hurt Hosea. Heartbroken, Hosea raised the children by himself and desperately missed the wife that he loved yet remained faithful to her in every way day after day. After a period of time God returned to Hosea and told him to go out in search of Gomer to bring her back home. Hosea found his wife in all her wickedness and sin and ended up having to purchase her at an auction and brought her back where he continued to love her and tend to her needs and then she eventually changed to become pure, humble and honest before him. So it literally cost him to repurchase her to be his wife again. Has it cost you anything to love someone that hurt you?

God uses this peculiar story to illustrate the unfailing love that He has for His people. They, like Gomer, had turned their backs on God. They, like Gomer, proved themselves unfaithful to their commitment to God. With insignificance and willful intention they resumed their old lifestyle which did not honor God or obey his laws. Hosea mirrors the consistency of God's love for us just like we are called to do for our hurting spouse that treated us with disdain, disrespect and every evil thing. Hosea 14:4 NKJV says, *"I will heal their backsliding, I will love them freely, For My anger has turned away from him."*

Did Gomer deserve that kind of forgiveness? Do we or our spouse? God's love extends beyond the limits of our sinful humanity. He longs to draw us into a state of restoration with Himself. Just as He wants us to do for our spouse who may even be controlled by the spirit of Jezebel. However, merciful God that He is, adds this critical condition to His mercy in Hosea 5:15 NKJV, *"[15] I will return again to My place until they acknowledge their offense.*

Then they will seek My face; In their affliction they will earnestly seek Me."

The love of Hosea for his wife reminds us that the foremost fruit of the Spirit is love (Galatians 5:22). "The love of God has been poured out in our hearts by the Holy Spirit who was given to us" (Roman 5:5).

Loving someone that has wronged us is what we are called to do. Not to hold grudges or take offenses against them. We have no right no matter what someone else does to hurt us to ever hold unforgiveness against them as it will only hurt us and can cause infirmities and disease in our bodies. Every divorce today occurs because of unforgiveness and taking offenses by one person over another. Yes, there are many people that control and abuse their spouses to the point that they feel they have to leave just to survive and that is very unfortunate. I would never encourage divorce ever and only agree with physical separation with the goal of meeting together with someone that is Holy Spirit filled and discerning that understands how evil spirits affect people; and then work towards deliverance in order to save the marriage relationship. I have personally seen marriage after marriage saved when delivering one of the spouses from the Jezebel spirit.

So what Hosea did for Gomer is a model for what we are called to do for our spouses. Even though they may treat us disrespectfully and may even have relations with someone else or treat us horribly in every way imaginable – we are to love them and forgive them endlessly and desire for them to repent and change and get their life right with the Lord. If Hosea can do it, so can you. It will not be easy – but who said being a Christian means we get to enjoy living a life of ease with no persecution or tribulations. It can be extremely hard and painstaking in our hearts to love someone that hurts us in such deep ways that it is sometimes unimaginable to ever forgive. Take no offense ever no matter what the person does to you or says about you. Be quick to forgive so that no root of bitterness has a chance to grow in you and cause you to develop anger, hatred and all sorts of evil. That is the love that Christ loved the church with and called us to lay our own lives down for. You can do it. As you love them like Christ you will become more like Christ every day, month and year that you endure and do not give up on them. You can do it and you must do it all for the glory of God. God will bless you greatly for your personal sacrifice to help another come to Him. Do not take this assignment of your life lightly. The enemy will do everything he can to get you to abandon your tremendous act of extraordinary love. Do not let him win!

Chapter 9

What Did Jesus Do?

When most people think about the sacrifice that Jesus made for us in giving his life on the cross to atone for our sins, they know it was an extreme act giving up of one's own life for another. The fact that He had no sin at all and loved perfectly, yet was treated in the most horrible way possible as depicted in the movie *The Passion of the Christ* is nothing short of unbelievable. Have you ever thought about the amount of power that was available to Christ when the soldiers came to capture Him? John 18:4-6 states, "[4] Jesus therefore, knowing all things that would come upon Him, went forward and said to them, 'Whom are you seeking?' [5] They answered Him, 'Jesus of Nazareth.' Jesus said to them, 'I am He.' And Judas, who betrayed Him, also stood with them. [6] Now when

He said to them, 'I am He,' they drew back and fell to the ground." There were about 300 to 600 soldiers that were flattened by the supernatural power that was released by Jesus' words. Notice how Jesus identified Himself. He told them "I am He." These mighty words come from the Greek words "ego eimi," which is more accurately translated, "I AM!" It was not the first time Jesus used this phrase to identify Himself as He also used it in John 8:58 and John 13:19. When the hearers of that day heard those words ego eimi, they most certainly immediately recognized them as the very words God used to identify Himself when He spoke to Moses on Mount Horeb in Exodus 3:14. Then the power that was behind those words knocked everyone flat to the ground. Can you imagine what the soldiers were thinking after they fell to the ground? They all knew that this man had power in Him and could not be captured unless Jesus allowed himself to be.

The fact that Jesus had twelve legions of angels at His disposal when Judas brought the soldiers and officials of the chief priests and elders to come capture Him - have you ever thought about the power that He had that would have taken Him just a word to speak and He would have not have had to go through one of the most painful agonizing deaths possible?

Matthew 26:47-56 NKJV states, "[47] And while He was still speaking, behold, Judas, one of the twelve, with a great multitude with swords and clubs, came from the chief priests and elders of the people. [48] Now His betrayer had given them a sign, saying, 'Whomever I kiss, He is the One; seize Him.' [49] Immediately he went up to Jesus and said, 'Greetings, Rabbi!' and kissed Him. [50] But Jesus said to him, 'Friend, why have you come?' Then they came and laid hands on Jesus and took Him. [51] And suddenly, one of those who were with Jesus stretched out his hand and drew his sword, struck the servant of the high priest, and cut off his ear. [52] But Jesus said to him, 'Put your sword in its place, for all who take the sword will perish by the sword. [53] Or do you think that I cannot now pray to My Father, and He will provide Me with more than twelve legions of angels? [54] How then could the Scriptures be fulfilled, that it must happen thus?' [55] In that hour Jesus said to the multitudes, 'Have you come out, as against a robber, with swords and clubs to take Me? I sat daily with you, teaching in the temple, and you did not seize Me. [56] But all this was done that the Scriptures of the prophets might be fulfilled.' Then all the disciples forsook Him and fled."

What I wanted to impress upon you as you read this scripture was the ability of Jesus to simply speak a word and He could have avoided all of what was about to be done to Him which He knew would be horrifying in every way. Just what amount of power was available to Him at that point? There was no human force on earth that could match up to what Christ had available to Him – and to have twelve legions of angels that would have rescued Him if He just requested it yet He chose not to. Therefore the only way that He would be taken is if He allowed Himself to be taken. That is why He later told Pilate in John 19:11 NKJV, "Jesus answered, 'You could have no power at all against Me unless it had been given you from above. Therefore the one who delivered Me to you has the greater sin.'"

So what is a legion? The word "legion" is a military term that was taken from the Roman army and meant a group of at least 6,000 Roman soldiers, although the total number could be higher. Therefore in Mark 5:9 where the demon-possessed man of the Gadarenes had a legion of demons in him meant he had at least 6,000 of them controlling him inside. So since the word legion equates to at least 6,000 and Jesus said that the Father would give Him 'more than' twelve legions of angels if He requested it, then He would have had at least 72,000 angels that would have been given over to Him to provide him security and protection!

So just how powerful is one angel? In Isaiah 37:36 it states, "Then the angel of the Lord went out, and killed in the camp of the Assyrians one hundred and eighty-five thousand; and when people arose early in the morning, there were the corpses – all dead." So if one angel could kill 185,000 men in one night, how much combined strength and power would be in one legion of angels? One legion of angels could kill 1.11 billion people. Now multiply that times twelve legions and you would have the power to wipe out 13.3 billion people at Jesus' disposal which is almost twice the number of people living in the world right now. At the time Christ walked the earth there were only around 300 million people living.

Therefore, Jesus just had to say the word and He could have obliterated the Roman soldiers and the temple police that came to arrest him. Yet He chose to restrain the power that He possessed in order to allow the men to capture Him and ultimately kill Him in a most extreme and horrifying way.

God so loved the world that He gave His only begotten Son who willingly laid down His own life for all of us. If Christ did that for all of us and had no sin, how much more should we be willing to take verbal and emotional torment from a person who was hurt from their father and/or mother in order to show them love that they have never received in their lives to bring about an ultimate change and deliverance from the bondage they have been in their entire lives?

If we are to become like Christ, and love like Christ and lay our lives down for another, then that means that we need to be willing to show restraint with our own mouths and stop being pulled into strife from the enemy within our spouses, or children. They are simply being used by the enemy to torment us and we cannot ever allow ourselves to be drawn into strife. Would you ever see Christ getting into an argument with another person? The Pharisees and Sadducees tried pulling Him into a trap, but Christ showed tremendous restraint when engaging with "the enemy" within them and outsmarted them with discerning their disingenuous intentions and replying in calm wisdom every time. He knew that they were vipers and had hatred and jealousy in their hearts for Him yet He also knew He could not lose His cool and be pulled down to their level. He had to rise above the situation and stay in control.

So the next time your stepchild or child says something back to you that is disrespectful – use restraint and wisdom in responding back and do not be pulled into an argument because a servant of the Lord must not strive – ever. If your spouse comes at you and raises his or her voice to give you a verbal barrage – respond in peace and if you need to get away from them – tell them you need to go to the bathroom or you need to make a quick phone call and go to prayer and bind the enemy from them and then come back together when they are calmer.

When one thinks about the explosive power that Jesus had at his disposal and all He had to do was to say a word – He displayed the amazing sacrificial love that He was able to give to everyone in the world all the way to the end of His earthly life. When you are dealing with a person that you know is clearly in the wrong but they are doing so out of misdirection and pain in their life – look at them like Christ would have seen them and show compassion back to them. It is not easy – but it can and needs to be done.

When we think about how Christ knew everything and yet had to endure lowering himself to this world of humans and all our preconceived wrong ideas and change us to His perfect wisdom – just think how He had to restrain His words that His flesh might have wanted Him to speak out of exasperation to His disciples and others He met day to day. Think about how many times that He probably became annoyed with Peter and the other disciples and at times just wanted to speak His mind to them. He was especially not pleased with the Jewish leaders of the day knowing their hearts that were full of pride and arrogance. The only time the Bible ever records an act of aggression in Him was when He entered the temple courts and drove out all who were buying and selling there – shoving over the tables and benches of the money changers. He could no longer stand to watch a place that should have been revered operate as a marketplace of disrespect. Other than that He kept His emotions intact and under control at all times - which when you think about how challenging that would have been to do is nothing short of amazing.

Jesus discerned the heart of those He was speaking to and knew if they were sinning out of pain. If they were, then He was gentle and loving with His words. If they had hardened their hearts and were acting like they were above all others in piety and should have known better, then He would usually be more firm in His message. Therefore He had a shorter level of tolerance for those who were hypocrites. So we must have the same level of discernment in understanding who we are speaking with and what instruction we give them and how we convey a message to them. If they have been hurt by their father treating them poorly or they suffered through a divorce of their parents when they were just five or six years old, then it is important to know why they are behaving like they are because they can be acting out of the tremendous pain they are in and really need someone who they can talk to that is safe and loving in every way. When we have the compassion of Christ we see them differently and they receive us much more readily than when we are responding in our flesh with harshness.

Perhaps you know of pastors at a church who act like they love people while treating true victims of abuse with disdain such as a man who is married to a controlling wife that treats him like Jezebel. The Lord would not be pleased with pastors feeling sorry for the woman who has been abusing her husband and protecting her while being rude and kicking out the true victim. There is a thing called "righteous anger" and when a pastor who is supposed to be loving everyone as Christ treats someone who was already abused greatly with even more harshness and wrong judgment - then the Lord will fight that battle and correct the pastors for their unjust treatment - although it may take many months or even a year or longer for the pastors to be held accountable and the truth of the matter to be exposed. Trust in the Lord that all sin that is hidden will come out and He will stand up and protect those who have been wronged eventually. The Lord will fight your battles for you and correct those who are in the wrong. It is important as a pastor to hear the Lord and use discernment and wisdom when loving people like Christ and holding people accountable for actions and words.

So while Christ was not married to anyone nor had any children or stepchildren – He did model for us how to treat everyone appropriately. He had compassion for the broken hearted and healed their emotional pains by showing them unconditional love as he knew why they were behaving the way they did. He could see who they really were and that had they not been hurt by the enemy through other people in their lives then they would have been loving and patient. He loved all those who had physical infirmities and healed them wherever he visited as long as they came forward and had enough faith to believe that they would be healed. He lovingly corrected those living in sin as He did with the woman at the well who had multiple husbands and was living with a man that was not her husband. He even got angry at those in His Father's temple who were using it as a filthy marketplace and cleaned them out so they would keep His father's house holy. He had discernment over a person and situation and listened to His Father as to what needed to be done and that is exactly what we need to do in order to know how to react to various situations. We must do the same thing as Christ did in order to bring as many to Christ as possible before it is too late as time is getting closer every year. We must choose to love like Christ did wherever we go and whomever comes into our lives. The Lord is counting on us to help bring in the greatest harvest this world has ever seen and it is up to us to love everyone like Christ loved the church. Time is growing short and His return is nearing every day that goes past in your life. Therefore, please do not waste your time and help as many as you can come to Christ before it is too late!

Chapter 10

What Did Paul Do?

The last person the Lord wanted me to focus on who lived a life of sacrificial love was Paul – formally Saul. There is much we can learn from the life of Paul. He was far from ordinary as he was given the opportunity to do extraordinary things for the kingdom of God. The life of Paul is a story of redemption in Jesus Christ and a testimony that no one is beyond the saving grace of the Lord. However, to understand the full extent of this man we must first examine his dark side and what he symbolized before becoming the Apostle of Grace. Paul's early life was marked by religious zeal, brutal violence, and the relentless persecution of the early church.

Paul was born as Saul. Saul came from the Hebrew name (Sha'ul) which meant "asked for" or "prayed for." This was the name of the first king of Israel who ruled just before King David.

Saul was born in Tarsus in Cilicia around A.D. 1-5 in a province in the southeastern corner of modern day Tersous, Turkey. He was of Benjamite lineage and Hebrew ancestry. His parents were Pharisees – fervent Jewish nationalists who were very strict in staying to the Law of Moses – who sought to protect their children from "contamination" from the Gentiles. Anything Greek was despised in Saul's household, yet he could speak fluent Greek and passable Latin. His household spoke Aramaic, a derivative of Hebrew, which was the official language of Judea. Saul's family was considered to be Roman citizens but viewed Jerusalem as a truly sacred and holy city.

At age thirteen Saul was sent to Palestine to learn from a rabbi named Gamaliel, under whom Saul mastered Jewish history, the Psalms and the works of the prophets. His education would continue for five or six years as Saul learned such things as dissecting Scripture. It was during this time that he developed a question-and-answer style known in ancient times as "diatribe." This method of articulation helped rabbis debate the finer points of Jewish law to either defend or prosecute those who broke the law. Saul went on to become a lawyer, and all signs pointed to his becoming a member of the Sanhedrin, the Jewish Supreme Court of 71 men who ruled over Jewish life and religion. Saul was very zealous for his faith, and this faith did not allow for compromise. Thus it was this zeal that led him down the path of religious extremism.

It was this extremism that might have caused Saul to have been present at the trial of Stephen. He was present for his stoning and death and he held the garments of those who did the stoning (Acts 7:58). In Acts 5:27-42, Peter delivered his defense of the gospel and of Jesus in front of the Sanhedrin, which Saul heard. Gamaliel also was present and delivered a message to calm the council and stop them from stoning Peter. From that moment on Saul became even more determined to eliminate Christians as he watched the Sanhedrin flog Peter and others. Saul became more vigilant than ever to kill Christians as he felt he was doing it in the name of God. Obviously, when someone believes he is doing the work of God but in actuality is being used by the enemy, there is no one more vicious to live under for innocent people. Acts 8:3 NKJV states "As for Saul, he made havoc of the church, entering every house, and dragging off men and women, committing them to prison."

So what caused Saul to change so dramatically into the man who wrote most of the New Testament? When he met Jesus Christ on the road to Damascus! It was a journey of about 150 miles and part way there he was hit with a bright light and heard a voice stating, "Saul, Saul, why are you persecuting me?" Then Saul replied, "Who are you Lord?" of which Jesus answered, "I am Jesus, whom you are persecuting." Some scholars have suggested that a young Saul may have actually witnessed the death of Christ so he could have realized that the man that he saw die on the cross was now speaking to him.

From this moment on, Saul's life was forever changed as he was now blind and needed to depend on those who were around him. He was told by Jesus to continue on to Damascus and meet a man named Ananias who was hesitant to meet him due to his reputation of killing Christians. But the Lord told Ananias that Saul was His "chosen instrument" to carry His name before the Gentiles. So he obeyed, laid his hands on him and Saul got his sight back was baptized and then received the Holy Spirit. Saul become Paul at that moment and went into the synagogues proclaiming Jesus and saying He was the Son of God. The people were amazed and skeptical because of his former reputation. The Jews were confused due to Paul's arguments now proving that Jesus was the Christ.

As a result of this miraculous transformation, Paul spent time in Arabia, Damascus, Jerusalem and Syria and Barnabas signed up to help him teach those in the church of Antioch. Paul ultimately wrote Romans, 1 and 2 Corinthians, Galatians, Ephesians, Philippians, 1 and 2 Thessalonians, Philemon, Colossians, 1 and 2 Timothy and Titus.

Paul lived a life of tremendous sacrifice for Christ - being beaten, stoned, dead, brought back to life, shipwrecked, jailed, left for dead and then assumed to die a martyr's death in the mid-to-late 60's A.D. in Rome. Loving people like Christ loved the church involves giving up our own selfish desires in order to help those who are selfish, unwise and in pain so that they can be changed, delivered and saved. Paul was forceful and fiery, so the Lord made sure he had plenty of trials that would test his patience and produce longsuffering to change him into who he really was in Christ. Paul

110

was harsh and judgmental, so God ensured that his many painful experiences would tenderize him into who he was in Christ. Paul could easily be full of pride and arrogance, so God squeezed the pride out of him. Paul knew that God was aware of what He was doing and that His intentions were only good, so readily accepted all that he had to endure in the transformation process. This is the same reason why the Lord puts people in our paths who are hard to love because it helps us to change into who we really should become in Christ.

So what do we learn from the life of Paul? First, we learn that God can save anyone. The remarkable story of Paul repeats itself every day as sinful, broken people all over the world are transformed by God's saving grace in Jesus Christ. Some of these people have done horrible and abusive things to other humans causing great suffering for years and years. When we read the story of Paul and know what he did for others, it is difficult for us to believe that God would allow into heaven religious extremists who murder innocent women and children. Today we see people on death row as unworthy of redemption because their crimes against humanity are just too great. Yet we live our lives in a sinful manner, expecting that God will be impressed by the fact that we have never killed anyone. The life of Paul is an example that every person matters to God, from the good, average person to the wicked and evil degenerate. Only God can save a soul from hell but he needs people like you and me that can love those who are suffering in great pain from their past. So that requires us to suffer through pain as they take it out on us.

Second, we learn from the story of Paul that anyone can become a humble, powerful witness for Jesus Christ. No other human figure in the Bible exhibited more humility while sharing the gospel of Jesus Christ as Paul. Acts 20:19 states that he "served the Lord with all humility and with tears and with trials that happened to him through the plots of the Jews." So expect to suffer tears and go through trials of injustice and then count it all as joy. It is what a Christian must go through if we are to follow in the steps of Christ. If Paul could endure what he did – then so can we. Do not complain when you are enduring the trial because the longer you complain the longer you will stay in that season of your life. It is not easy; but it is not supposed to be easy either because we are transforming from our selfish nature of the flesh into the selfless nature of the spirit. Glory to God in the highest as your transformation matures to completion.

Chapter 11

Can Christians Have Demons?

During my experience of seeing people who are called to love on those that have been hurt (mainly by their spouses or stepchildren) I have met many of these hurting people who are Spirit-filled Christians and many that have their prayer language but manifest behavior that is anything but loving and pure. I have been director of the Healing Rooms at New Life Assembly of God in Noblesville since October of 2015 and have worked with many people who have treated their spouses in ways that are not consistent with a loving and caring godly person. While they do have a desire to serve the Lord and they do at times hear clearly from the Lord they also hear from the enemy frequently and exhibit behavior that is extremely controlling, manipulative and evil which always begs the question -are they really true Christians? Can a Christian hear from the Lord and be tormented by the enemy at the same time to behave in ways contrary to the Lord? Absolutely they can and do all the time as it is a process of becoming free from enemy spirits as well as renewing their minds from things that the enemy did to them to cause them to be hurt. Just because you give your life to the Lord and ask Him to be Lord of your life does not mean that every affecting tormenting demonic spirit automatically leaves you. You have to take authority and command the spirits to be gone and it may be a process of months or even years before you become aware of what needs to be done to be completely free. I have worked with many people who have prayed the renunciation prayers in my *Restored to Freedom* book to get set free from the spirit of Jezebel, Leviathan and others. Many have felt the spirits go instantly and some even felt they were being choked as the spirits were leaving them. All those who had received total deliverance stated that they felt the heaviness of the spirits go from them as they felt so much lighter in their body. It was like the chains that were on their shoulders had been removed and they felt so much cleaner and much more pure, many for the first time. So, yes, Christians absolutely can have demons inside of them that are tormenting them to behave in ways that are not Christ-like. I love the way that John Eckhardt explains this sometimes confusing situation:

> There was a time when we taught in our church that Christians could not have demons. I preached long sermons stating that Christians could be oppressed, regressed, digressed, obsessed and suppressed, but never possessed. We believed that a demon could be outside a Christian oppressing him but that it could not be inside him. The reasoning I used to defend this position was that Jesus and the Holy Spirit could not live inside the same body in which demons reside.

> The problem was, our experience did not match our theology. When we ministered deliverance, we frequently prayed for people we knew were born-again, Spirit-filled believers--and

114

they manifested demons! We had to face the fact that either our experience was wrong or our doctrine was wrong.

We could not question our experience because we knew what we were seeing. So we began to question our theology.

In our search for truth, we realized that in the Bible, Jesus tells us to cast devils out, not to cast devils off. Obviously, for something to come out, it must be in. We finally came to the conclusion that our interpretation of the Bible had been wrong.

Now I am convinced not only that a Christian can have demons but also that there are demons that operate in the realm of theology, encouraging us to argue and debate endlessly over doctrine rather than meeting the needs of people who are hurting. Demons actually help promote the teaching that a Christian cannot have a demon, because they gain strength from staying hidden. They can operate in their destructive ways without being challenged!

Some may argue that a believer cannot be possessed. But the dismaying fact remains that born-again Christians, including leaders, are experiencing difficulties that can find no solution in natural infirmities or the endless conflict between the flesh and the Spirit.

It's time to acknowledge that we are dealing with real people who have real problems and that God did not save and commission us so we could argue over doctrine. He called us into ministry so we can help people who are hurting, wounded and bruised.

When you come into contact with someone who is controlled by demons, the answer is to cast the devils out, not to argue about whether or not the person is a Christian. The answer is to bring help to that person.

Possessed or Not Possessed?

I realize I'm not the only believer who has ever had an erroneous idea about Christians being possessed. And the sensationalized picture Hollywood has painted of demon possession has not helped. It has led us to believe that if we say a Christian can be possessed, we are saying he can be fully owned and controlled by the devil and will manifest, Hollywood-style, with head spinning and eyes popping out.

The word "possessed" is an unfortunate translation because it connotes ownership, and we know that the devil cannot own a Christian--that is, have complete control of him. But in the Bible, there is no real distinction between being possessed and being oppressed, digressed, suppressed, obsessed and so forth. All these terms mean that a person is, to some degree, under the influence of a demon.

Personally, I do not have as much of a problem with the word "possessed" as other Christians do. In fact, to me the word "demonized" sounds worse.

When I looked up "possess" in the dictionary, I discovered that one definition of the word is "to occupy." My contention is that if a demon occupies your big toe, he possesses that part of you. It doesn't mean he possesses your spirit, soul and body. But if he occupies even a small portion, such as a physical organ in your body--as a spirit of infirmity does--then there is possession to some degree.

I often ask those who are skeptical of demon possession whether or not cancer is demonic. Most will agree that sickness is of the devil.

So then, I continue, is cancer inside the body, or is there something on the outside that's the problem? If it isn't on the inside, doctors probably wouldn't cut people open trying to remove it. Evidently, as a Christian, you can have something in you that is possessing a certain organ of your body and is not of God.

Knowing that a Christian can be possessed (or demonized) in some part of his being raises the question: Is any part off-limits to demons? Here is where we can reconcile the issue of Jesus and the Holy Spirit residing simultaneously within someone who needs deliverance.

One thing that has helped us in our understanding is the realization that every person is made up of three parts: spirit, soul and body. When Jesus comes into a believer's life, He comes into that person's spirit. John 3:6 tells us clearly, "That which is born of the Spirit is spirit" (NKJV). A demon cannot dwell in a Christian's spirit because that is where Jesus and the Holy Spirit dwell.

It is the other components that make up a human being--the soul (mind, will and emotions) and the body--that are the targets of demonic attack. Demons can dwell in those areas of a Christian's life. So when we say that a Christian is demonized or possessed, we are not saying he has a demon in his spirit but in some part of his soul or body.

To illustrate this truth, the Lord reminded us of the biblical account of Jesus' going into the temple and cleansing it of thieves and moneychangers. The Greek word used for "drove out" in this account is ekballo, which means "to expel or drive out." It is the same word that is used in Mark 16:17: "In My [Jesus'] name they will cast out demons."

We know that according to the Bible God's children are the temple of the Spirit of God (see 1 Cor. 3:16). In the Old Testament the temple had three parts: the holy of holies, the holy place and the outer court. This picture is a type or representation of who we are as His temple today.

The shekinah glory of God, or God's "presence," was in the holy of holies. This part of the temple represents our spirits.

But when Jesus went into the temple to drive out the thieves and moneychangers, He did not go into the holy of holies. He went into the outer court, where these evildoers were carrying on their business transactions.

The whole account is a picture of deliverance--of what Jesus wants to do in our temples. There may be demonic thieves in our lives that are operating in our outer courts (bodies or souls).

117

Even though they cannot enter the holy of holies (our spirits), Jesus wants them expelled because the temple of God was never intended to be a place for thieves to operate. It is meant to be a place of worship and a place of prayer.

A Covenant Right

Those who believe that the ministry of deliverance is not for believers need to reconsider their position. The truth is, rather, that deliverance is not for the unbeliever.

What good would it do to cast demons out of an unbeliever, unless he is planning to get saved? Unbelievers cannot maintain their deliverance. In fact, according to Luke 11:24-26, after undergoing deliverance, the unsaved person is subject to receiving seven times as many demons as he had before.

The ministry of deliverance is the covenant right of believers. Like every other blessing from God--healing, prosperity, miracles and so on--it is promised only to His covenant people, those who believe in Jesus and come to God through Christ's blood. God, in His mercy, will bless people outside the covenant because He is merciful. But primarily, His blessings are based on covenant.

The story of the Syrophoenician woman in Mark 7:25-30 makes this clear. The woman sought out Jesus so He would deliver her daughter from an unclean spirit. But Jesus told her, "'Let the children be filled first, for it is not good to take the children's bread and throw it to the little dogs'" (v. 27).

In this verse, the phrase "the children's bread" refers specifically to deliverance, and Jesus is saying it belongs to His covenant people. Those outside the covenant may receive a miracle based on God's mercy, but deliverance is meant for those who have a covenant with God.

Luke 1:71-73 says Jesus came "that we should be saved from our enemies and from the hand of all who hate us, to perform the mercy promised to our fathers and to remember His holy covenant, the oath which He swore to our father Abraham." He brought salvation from our enemies--devils and demons--based on a promise, of which we are heirs (see Gal. 3:29), that He made to Abraham.

The purpose of this salvation is stated in subsequent verses of Luke 1: "To grant us that we, being delivered from the hand of our enemies, might serve Him without fear, in holiness and righteousness before Him, all the days of our life" (vv. 74-75). God provides the benefit so that we may serve Him without fear, in holiness and in righteousness all the days of our lives. It is very difficult to live this way without being delivered. In fact, it is practically impossible.

One of the reasons it is so difficult is that demons are not always a result of sin in a person's life. There are many different kinds of evil spirits, and not all of them are what I refer to as "spirits of sin."

That is not to say that sin is not a huge entry point for demonic influence. For every sin in the Bible there is a corresponding demon. I maintain that if a Christian is living in sin or living in the flesh, there's no way he can escape demons.

However, it is also possible for a Christian to be demonized as a result of someone else's sin. For instance, a spirit of rejection or trauma can come upon a person because he is abused. Or demons may be inherited from a previous generation through a person's bloodline.

We have come a long way in our church since the early days when we believed Christians could not have demons. Now whenever a person gets saved, we automatically assume he needs some level of deliverance, and we lead him through the process. We don't question if the new believer has a demon, only how many he has.

That may sound hard. But remember, demonization is not always the person's own fault. Generational issues are a major entry point.

If we can be subjected to the consequences of sin to the fourth generation, as Exodus 20:5 says, and a biblical generation is 40 years, then we are subject to the demonic influence of what people in our family lines were doing 160 years before us. This means that, taking the year 2000 as a starting point, we are affected by what those in our bloodlines were doing as far back as the year 1840.

Think about it. Even if a person has a great genealogy, he can't know everything his ancestors were doing in secret that long ago. And if, in addition to generational sin, he has committed personal sin or has been traumatized or victimized in any way, by the time he comes to the Lord, he is going to need deliverance on some level. There is just too much defilement and contamination on Earth to escape it.

We must accept the reality that we have been commissioned to minister to God's covenant people, and part of our responsibility is to provide them with their covenant right of deliverance. If we deprive them of it based on some erroneous theological doctrine, then we are denying them what is rightfully theirs, and we cannot call ourselves able ministers of the New Covenant. Let's do as Jesus did, and serve the children's bread to those who need it!

I believe that John did a great job of articulating the understanding of how people today are affected and afflicted with demonic spirits that cause them to behave in ways that are not godly and give them physical afflictions that are painful. I believe that if we as Christians are not at peace than there is a demonic influence causing it. Thus, if we are thinking about our finances and how we might not be able to pay for a certain bill on time, then a spirit of fear is causing us to be in worry and fear. We can then command it to go and will get our peace back. If we are reading a book to our self and our spouse comes walking into the room and speaks out words that are hurtful – it is a spirit in them that is causing them to be mean, controlling or whatever – and that spirit is trying to cause conflict and hurt you. If only all could see into the spiritual realm and discern what is going on inside of a person, then everyone would know without a shadow of a doubt why a person is behaving in ways that are not easy to love. Unfortunately we have to look at the fruit in a person's life and often times that is the behavior that is prevalent and if the person behaves in an ungodly way and is mean, harsh and angry then there is a really good chance that the person is being influenced by the enemy.

Chapter 12

How to Love Like Christ

The last chapter is focused on what specific practical things a person can do on a day to day basis to love others like Christ called us to. Loving those who are easy to love takes no effort on our part other than to treat them like we would want to be treated. Therefore I am going to focus on what things we can do to love on those who are more challenging to enjoy and live with due to them being hurt by others in their lives. The most important thing is to discern what state of mind that the person is in that we are called to love. If the person simply cannot stay in peace much of their day to day life and causes arguments and strife the majority of the time, then the greater amount of grace will be required and the more irritation they will cause you. So for the sake of this section let's determine that the person we are describing is one that I will call "highly not fun" to be around (and I am sure you can think of some people in your life who this describes). These types of people will have had father wounds, possibly mother wounds and definitely relationship wounds from people who abandoned them or divorced them causing them even more rejection pain or they may have even been molested by someone. So what do you need to do on a day to day basis when living with these types of people?

1) **There but for the grace of God go I.** Keep your mind focused on how these people were hurt by their father and/or mother or other people in their lives and that they are simply acting out challenging behavior based on the pain in their lives. When you can think about this and understand that they are behaving in a hard to love manner due to their pain – it becomes much easier to love them without opening your mouth to criticize or condemn them. If you had endured the extreme trauma that they went through, then you could have been exactly like them. Show them grace.

2) **Pray for the eyes of Christ to see with.** When you can look at these people like Christ or God looks at them and see yourself as an agent of the Lord whose assignment is to help love on His hurting people that are hard to love and that the Lord will reward you for your sacrifice eternally and most likely here on earth, then it becomes easier to endure. You are literally being persecuted for the sake of Christ – sometimes by those who are Christians. So ask the Lord to give you His eyes to see them through and watch how you will be able to supernaturally change and be able to see them exactly as the Father sees them.

3) **Keep your mind to yourself.** It is important when interacting with people who have been hurt to keep yourself from speaking out loud what you are thinking if the enemy whispers to you. Just say "No" when it comes to wanting to speak your mind. Praying in tongues either in your mind or under your breath during times when they are provoking you helps you stay in peace tremendously because the enemy

123

cannot taunt you and tempt you to speak out words back to your perpetrator. Often times the hard to love person will know exactly what to say to hurt you the greatest because the enemy is speaking through them to you. So expect to receive some horrible verbal assaults and pray in tongues. I was once in the car and my son was speaking words that he should not have been so I started to pray in tongues and he literally got quiet because he had no idea what to say back! It was amazing and awesome to see that the enemy in him shut his mouth and actually did not talk the rest of the trip. If you do not have the gift of tongues, ask the Lord for it and He will give it to you. It is an amazing tool to have in your tool belt.

4) **Stay calm and part if you need to.** If the person is verbally attacking you then tell them politely that you need to step away. Make an excuse if you have to (go to the bathroom, make a quick call, go for a brief walk alone, ride your bike, run to the store, etc.) because the goal of the enemy in them is to draw you into an argument or beat you down to control you with their words. Do not speak to them and say, "I rebuke you in the name of Jesus" because that will escalate the anger that the spirit has inside of them towards you. Trust me on this one – as I have personal experience and have confirmed this with other people. As much as you are able you must stay calm and keep your peace in the midst of the storm and strife. You can tell them that what they are saying is hurting your heart and if the real person inside of them has any conscience they will back down and cease. If the enemy spirit is strong on them, nothing much will cause them to care about you and your welfare.

5) **Get out of Dodge pronto.** If the person you are trying to love on throws things such as knives, glasses, bottles, phones, etc near you or at you, then it is best to leave their presence immediately by getting out of the room, house or car. If they follow after you then you may need to obviously run faster to get away or call the police if you absolutely have no other choice. It is unfortunate if that occurs because once

124

the authorities are brought in the person may choose to lie about the situation and possibly even blame you for their actions unless you have witnesses. If you can run to other people either in the home or outside it is best because then the spirits on the person will have to behave.

6) **Pray for the patience of the Lord**. Typically the challenging people that you are choosing to love will not be at peace and usually will be very anxious and thus will be hard to be around because you will feel the fear and anxiety on them and it will often times drive you away from them. Ask the Lord for the supernatural ability to be patient with them and He will give you His perspective and vision to see them with and His compassion. Again, if you need to take a break from being around them due to their anxiety levels then tell them that you need to step away for 30-60 minutes and then you will come back. Also, if you do step away for more than this amount of time then text them so they feel at peace that you are not leaving them permanently; as most have felt rejection from their parents and relationships in the past and this can cause them to feel that pain again. It is tremendous torment for them and you need to show extreme compassion for them.

7) **Expect to spend money**. When others cost you money due to their mistakes you will need to stay calm and trust the Lord to provide for all your needs. Sometimes it may cost you hundreds of dollars, sometimes thousands of dollars, but whatever the cost – count it all joy and trust that the Lord will have your back and provide for you when you are in need. It can be very hard to bite your tongue on this issue because the enemy will whisper to you quite loudly as you spend your money and sacrifice your needs for others' foolish decisions. Yes, you need to use some wisdom on just what you pay for and how much – but again if the person you are loving has been hurt in extreme ways then they will make bad decisions that will usually cost money. Most people would suggest that we do not want to enable them and I would agree that we do not want to – but if the people have

been hurt in major ways by others then they are really incapable of making wise decisions. Obviously if the people are hurting themselves with their financial decisions you need to be wise and listen to the Lord as to what you should pay for. If the person is so depressed that they cannot even get a job and work – then understand that and behave accordingly. It is very important to hear the Lord on these decisions because you do not want to enable any drug addictions or sex addictions.

8) **Speak Life.** When you are working with a person who is hard to love, they will tend to speak very depressing words and hopelessness will exude from them. Try to change their words to those that bring life and are positive and uplifting. Shift their minds away from their negative circumstances onto things that bring them joy or encouragement. Let them know that things will not always be the same and try to refocus them on things from the Lord. Remind them of Philippians 4:8-9 NKJV, "[8] Finally brethren, whatever things are true, whatever things are noble, whatever things are just, whatever things are pure, whatever things are lovely, whatever things are of good report, if there is any virtue and if there is anything praiseworthy – meditate on these things. [9] The things which you learned and received and heard and saw in me, these do, and the God of peace will be with you." Therefore – try to get the people to think about good things and watch their countenance change for the positive.

9) **Confront in love.** What do you do if the people you are trying to love on lie to you consistently? The lies then make it very difficult to have a solid relationship with the person. This becomes a tough one because once you have lost trust that they are able to tell you the truth, you then cannot be sure if whatever they say to you is honest and thus you question them. Normally you can look into their eyes when they lie to you and you will be able to discern it. So what should you do when you catch them in a lie? Stay calm and let them know that it is not appropriate to lie to you because then you cannot trust them until they earn it back and that

could take days, weeks, months or years depending on how often they lie and their conscience for lying.

10) **Take no offense**. Tolerating annoying behaviors can be very hard to endure. Say that the person does not flush the toilet after they go and you have asked them to do it over and over. When they live in your home and it smells up your home – you could say that you will not do something for them until they flush (such as not make dinner or let them eat). But what if you are married to their mother and she is not able to make her own son do the honors? Then it becomes very challenging as she may feel guilty because their father divorced her and she feels sorry for him and even though she has asked him to take care of it, he was stuck at age 5 when his father left him and now at age 28 is still being affected. Perhaps your stepson had a baby out of wedlock and wants his mother (your wife) to babysit for him many times as it enables him to have fun instead of taking responsibility. Then it becomes a big challenge to endure what you know to be wrong while also trying to show compassion while not getting into strife with your wife. Pray about exactly what you should do and then do what the Lord tells you to do. Annoying behaviors can be very hard to correct because if you bring it up you could cause the person to take an offense against you even though they should not. They end up not apologizing and will do additional negative behavior to get back at you for confronting them. Suffering as unto the Lord may be necessary on your part for a season and it may take years to undo the damage that was done to that person the Lord has called you to love. Obviously, this is a challenge but trust that the Lord is watching and will bless you greatly for this sacrifice. Never ever, ever take an offense!

I think it is imperative to talk about the differences in various people in being able to tolerate those who are hard to love in life. Some people have no tolerance whatsoever for putting up with people who have issues in their life that cause them any annoyances. They are very selfish and have no care to get involved in the lives of those who have no value to them. For those types of people I am sad and the Lord is grieved because that is not an example of loving like Christ, nor is it the kind of attitude that we are called to perform. Still, there are many people in the business world who are all business and no compassion. I have personally met many of those types of people, and it is very sad because many of them need to be healed from wounds in their lives in order to have the proper compassion level to care for those truly hurting. They are very self-absorbed in their own worlds and when they pass from this world the Lord will ask them what they did for His kingdom; and unfortunately they will have little to show.

Then there are those who attend church regularly and tithe and want to help people as long as it does not involve any of their time personally. Again, these types of people try to appear good to those who know them on a surface level, but when it comes down to it they do not want to get their hands dirty nor get involved with dealing with people who are hard to love because it would just "cramp their style." We all know people like that in the church -- as there are many. Usually they like to attend larger churches where they can blend in and not have to be depended on to help the less fortunate personally with their time. They are fine with writing a check out and giving some money once in a while but when it involves suffering they are not able to, nor willing to endure unpleasant life situations. I would say the bulk of the Christian world includes these people, which if we could get more of these people to be more giving of their time, this world would be a much better place.

Finally, there are those who are like Mother Theresa or Heidi Baker – they truly care for those that are suffering and are willing to get involved and sacrifice their own comforts for others. They would be willing to lay down their own lives for others as they have the compassion of Christ; and while their rewards on earth may not show now, their rewards in heaven will be great for all eternity. I would even say that when a person is living in a situation willingly and absorbing tremendous verbal barrages that they may even have a leg up on those just serving the less fortunate who are truly grateful and easy to love on. When you are being disrespected, mocked, lied to, and treated like you are scum – and yet you still love those who are persecuting you – then the Lord greatly appreciates that tremendous personal sacrifice. You not only get your hands dirty but your heart and emotions take a beating from those you are trying to love on. There are few of these types of people, but my hope is that after people have read this book that there will be more who are willing to get involved with the hard to love. It will be worth it in the end even though it will be a challenge in the now. It may take more of your free time than what you would like, but the Lord will honor you and you will help more people get an eternal salvation which means everything to the Lord.

While enduring living with someone who causes you great stress and hardships is not fun or enjoyable – if you can see them as Christ sees them you will be able to make it through a challenging season of your life. If you can also see that by going through this sacrifice that you are having a positive effect on your own life by causing you to become more like Christ, then that is a major benefit because we all say that we want to be more like Christ yet when the Lord gives us a situation that causes us pain we then cry out to have it stop instead of saying "Thank you Lord as I count it all as joy."

Keep in mind that most of these seasons of sacrifice are exactly that – a season. And just like a season of nature – expect the season to change after a certain time frame once you have accomplished what the Lord intended you to do. It could be several months or years and sometimes it could be most of your life – but as long as you do not complain throughout the process the Lord will bless and honor you for helping out His people to be loved on unconditionally. Loving like Christ loved the church is not only possible – but also doable. As the large sportswear company in Oregon says....Just do it!

References

Mark Lane - Bible Numbers For Life
John Eckhardt – Why a Christian Can Have a Demon (Charisma Magazine)

Final Thoughts

The Lord has told me that everyone knows many in their lives who are unable to live in peace and that cause much strife. They are people they are married to, have children or stepchildren with, work with, or people with whom they attend church or other ministries. Please make your family and friends aware that they can endure living with someone who is challenging to love as it allows them to show Christ to them and helps to slowly change their own life to becoming more like Christ as well as those they are called to love on. The enemy is not you or your spouse or your children or stepchildren – the enemy is demonic spirits causing them to behave in ways that are not godly, nor loving, and especially not peaceful and contradictory to the true Holy Spirit.

There are millions and millions of people who have no idea they are being afflicted by demonic spirits out of fear, anger and hearing voices whisper to them to behave in ways that others do not want to be around. They are living miserable lives and causing misery to those who they should be loving. When you understand that those people who are hard to love are simply acting out based on the pain they have endured in their own lives, then you are able to see them as Christ sees them. They are wounded people who need extra love and patience and need you in their lives to help them get to the other side of their pain.

If you would like me to speak and minister at your church, seminar or conference you may contact me on my website. If the revelations in this book have helped you and changed your life or saved your marriage you may wish to make a tax deductible donation to Restored to Freedom at http://www.restoredtofreedom.com which will help continue to get the message out to people all over the world that there is hope and a way to gain total freedom in Jesus Christ. Amen.